THE U.S. GROUND WAR IN VIETNAM 1965–1973

VIETNAM WAR

THE U.S. GROUND WAR IN VIETNAM 1965–1973

MASON CREST

Mason Crest
450 Parkway Drive, Suite D
Broomall, PA 19008
www.masoncrest.com

© 2018 by Mason Crest, an imprint of National Highlights, Inc.

All rights reserved. No part of this publication may be reproduced or transmitted in any form or by any means, electronic or mechanical, including photocopying, recording, taping, or any information storage and retrieval system, without permission in writing from the copyright holder.

Cataloging-in-Publication Data on file with the Library of Congress.

Printed and bound in the United States of America.

First printing
9 8 7 6 5 4 3 2 1

ISBN: 978-1-4222-3890-5
Series ISBN: 978-1-4222-3887-5
ebook ISBN: 978-1-4222-7800-7
ebook series ISBN: 978-1-4222-7897-0

Produced by Regency House Publishing Limited
The Manor House
High Street
Buntingford
Hertfordshire
SG9 9AB
United Kingdom

www.regencyhousepublishing.com

Text copyright © 2018 Regency House Publishing Limited/Christopher Chant.

PAGE 2: A Viet Cong base on fire with Private First Class Raymond Rumpa in the foreground.

PAGE 3: Private First Class Russell R. Widdifield of 3rd Platoon, Company M, 3rd Battalion, 7th Marine Regiment, takes a break during a ground movement 25 miles (40km) north of An Hoa, North Vietnam.

RIGHT: A Marine stands watch in an observation tower as Lt. Commander McElroy, the 3rd Battalion, 26th Marines chaplain, holds mass on Hill 950.

PAGE 6: Troops of "A" Company, 1st Air Cavalry Division, checking house during patrol.

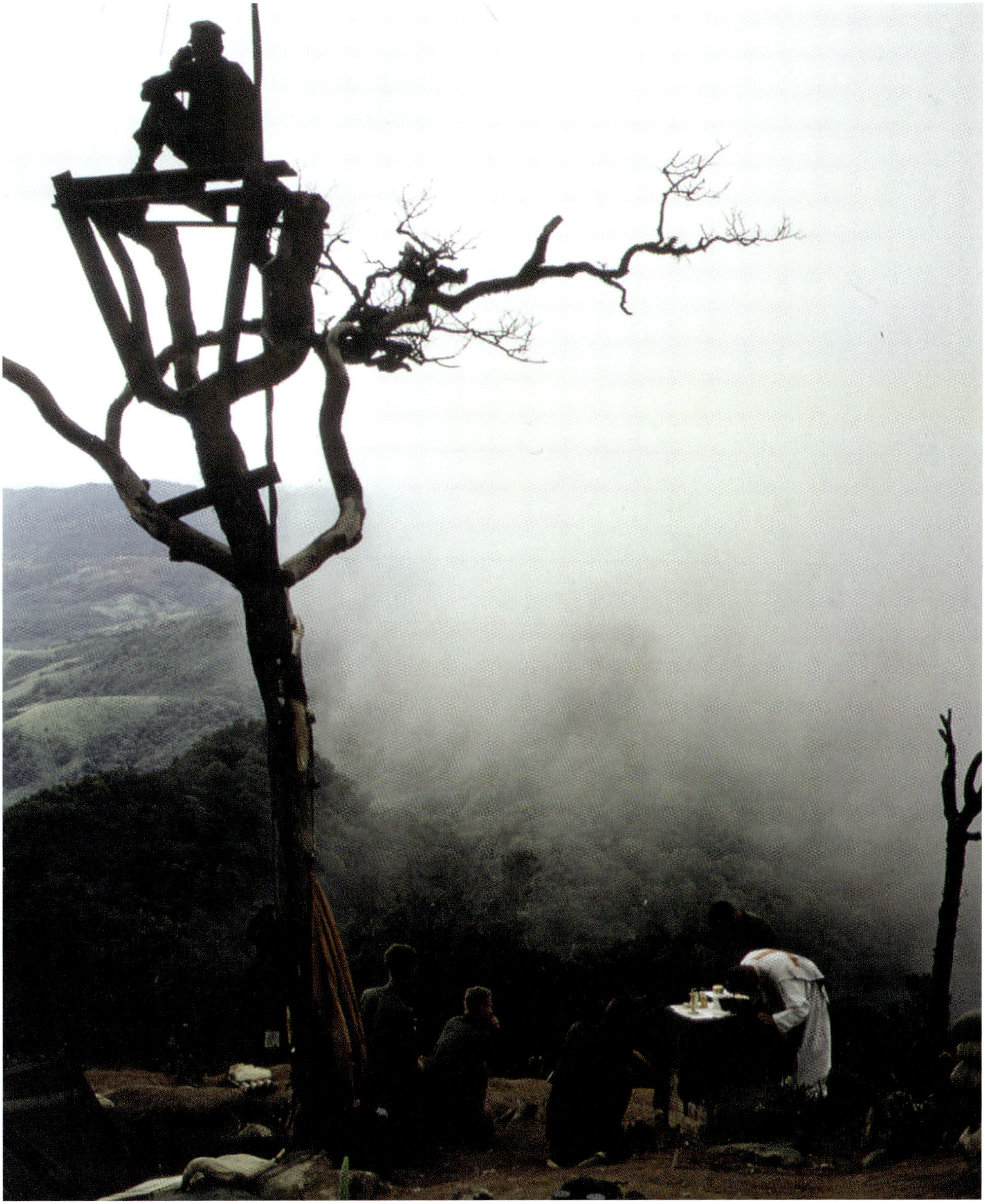

TITLES IN THE VIETNAM WAR SERIES:

**The Origins of Conflict in the Vietnam War
The Escalation of American Involvement in the Vietnam War
The U.S. Ground War in Vietnam 1965 –1973
Stalemate: U.S. Public Opinion of the War in Vietnam
The Fall of Saigon and the End of the Vietnam War**

CONTENTS

Vietnam Veterans Memorial 10

Chapter One:
The Fatal Commitment 12

Chapter Two:
America's First Major Offensive 34

Time Line of the Vietnam War 70

Series Glossary of Key Terms 72

Further Reading and Internet Resources 73

Index 76

Further Information 80

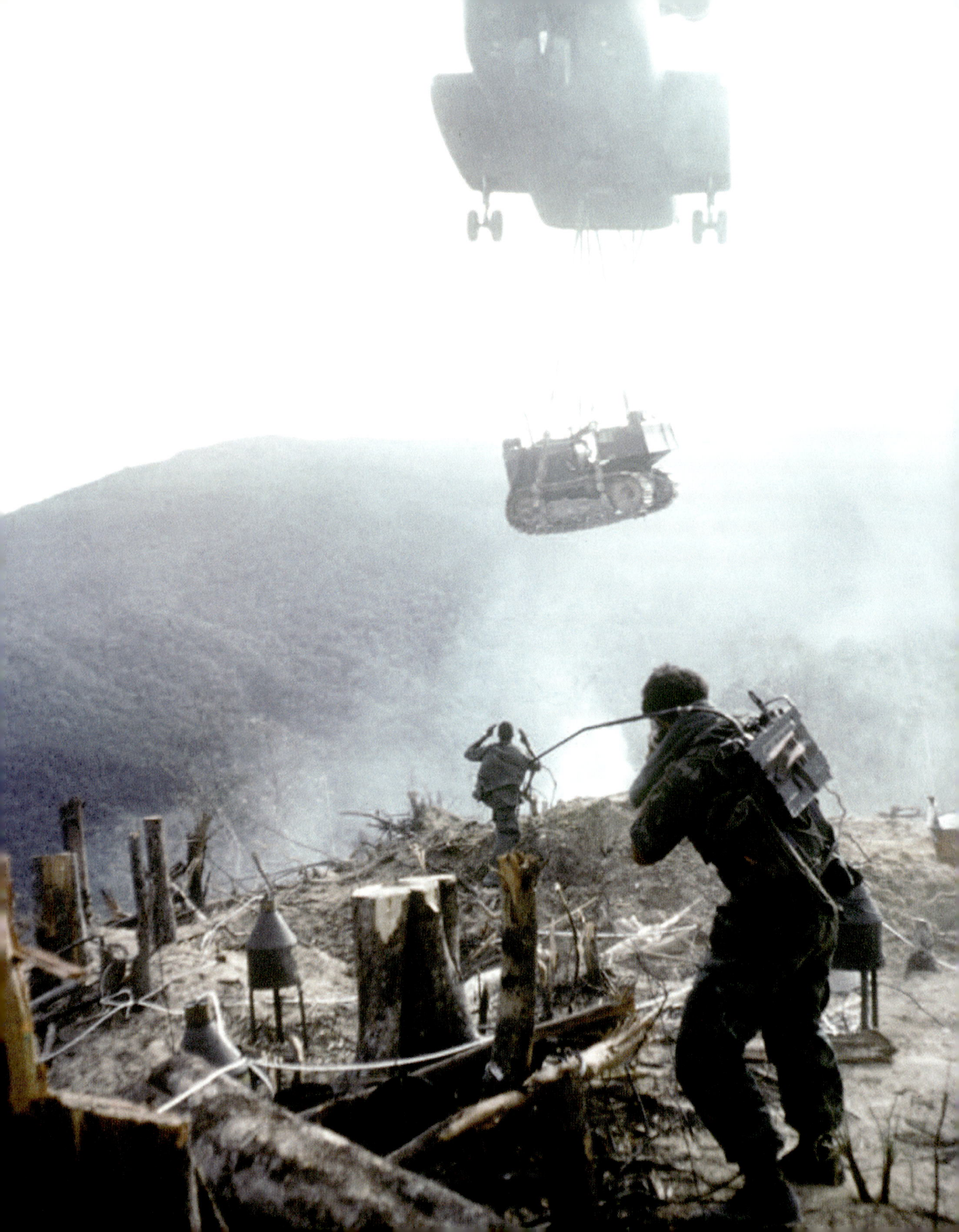

KEY ICONS TO LOOK FOR:

Words to Understand: These words with their easy-to-understand definitions will increase the reader's understanding of the text, while building vocabulary skills.

Sidebars: This boxed material within the main text allows readers to build knowledge, gain insights, explore possibilities, and broaden their perspectives by weaving together additional information to provide realistic and holistic perspectives.

Educational Videos: Readers can view videos by scanning our QR codes, providing them with additional content to supplement the text. Examples include news coverage, moments in history, speeches, iconic sports moments, and much more!

Text-Dependent Questions: These questions send the reader back to the text for more careful attention to the evidence presented here.

Research Projects: Readers are pointed toward areas of further inquiry connected to each chapter. Suggestions are provided for projects that encourage deeper research and analysis.

Series Glossary of Key Terms: This back-of-the-book glossary contains terminology used throughout the series. Words found here increase the reader's ability to read and comprehend high-level books and articles in this field.

OPPOSITE: A CH-53 Sea Stallion helicopter airlifts a bulldozer into a mountaintop fire support base construction site. The CH-53 is being guided in by members of a 3rd Marine Division construction team.

10

Vietnam Veterans Memorial

The Vietnam Veterans Memorial was designed by Maya Lin, a 21-year-old from Athens, Ohio. It was unveiled with an opening ceremony in 1982 in Washington, D.C.

The memorial is dedicated to the men and women in the U.S. military who served in the war zone of Vietnam. The names of the 58,000 Americans who gave their lives and service to their country are etched chronologically in gabbro stone and listed on the two walls which make up the memorial monument. Those who died in action are denoted by a diamond, those who were missing (MIAs, POWs, and others) are denoted with a cross. When the death of one, who was previously missing is confirmed, a diamond is superimposed over a cross.

The wall consists of two sections, one side points to the Lincoln Memorial and the other to the Washington Monument. There is a pathway along the base for visitors to walk and reflect, or view the names of their loved ones.

When visiting the memorial many take a piece of paper, and using a crayon or soft pencil make a memento of their loved one. This is known as "rubbing." The shiny wall was designed to reflect a visitor's face while reading the names of the military personnel who lost their lives. The idea is that symbolically the past and present are represented. The memorial was paid for by the Vietnam Veterans Memorial Fund, Inc. who raised nearly $9,000,000 to complete it.

The memorial site also includes The Three Servicemen statue built in 1984. The statue depicts three soldiers, purposefully identifiable as *European American, African American,* and *Hispanic American.* The statue faces the wall with the soldiers looking on in solemn tribute at the names of their fallen comrades.

The Vietnam Women's Memorial is dedicated to the women of the United States who served in the Vietnam War, most of whom were nurses. It serves as a reminder of the importance of women in the conflict.

The Vietnam Veterans Memorial can be found to the north of the Lincoln Memorial near the intersection of 22nd St. and Constitution Ave. NW. The memorial is maintained by the U.S. National Park Service, and receives approximately 5 million visitors each year. It is open 24 hours a day and is free to all visitors.

Chapter One
THE FATAL COMMITMENT

Even as Rolling Thunder was being fought in the skies over North Vietnam, the military situation on the ground in South Vietnam was deteriorating steadily and, it seemed, inevitably. At a time early in March 1965, the Military Assistance Command Vietnam (MACV) forecast was that if the current trends persisted, South Vietnamese strength would soon be confined to district and provincial capitals, which would be essentially unmanageable because of the huge numbers of refugees which would overwhelm local services and administrative capabilities. In his capacity as head of the MACV, General Westmoreland believed and said that South Vietnam could be wholly in Communist hands within 12 months.

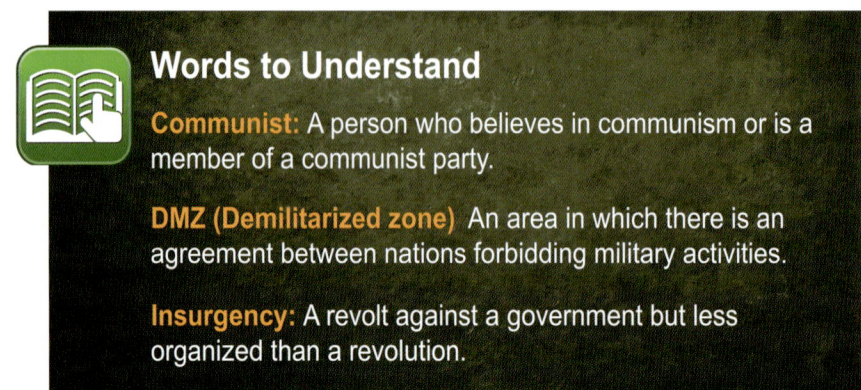

Early in 1965, therefore, the only hope of bringing the Communists to a halt, if not actually defeating them, seemed to lie not with the South Vietnamese ground forces, with limited U.S. technical and logistical support, but with U.S. air power striking deep into North Vietnam in Rolling Thunder, in the misconceived hope of persuading the North Vietnamese to negotiate, and of severing the lines of communication (in particular the portion of the Ho Chi Minh Trail in eastern Laos) by which the North Vietnamese were able to nourish and bolster the Communist ground effort in South Vietnam. In the light of the Communist attacks on the bases at Pleiku and Qui Nhon, however, Westmoreland had very little confidence in the ability of the South Vietnamese army to provide an effective defense of the airfields on which U.S. aircraft were based for the support of the selfsame South Vietnamese army. Westmoreland's intelligence staff estimated that no fewer than 12 Communist battalions, with 6,000 men, lay within striking distance of the air base at Da Nang, a large and crucially important facility containing large matériel dumps but protected by only a comparatively small and badly-trained South

> **Words to Understand**
>
> **Communist:** A person who believes in communism or is a member of a communist party.
>
> **DMZ (Demilitarized zone)** An area in which there is an agreement between nations forbidding military activities.
>
> **Insurgency:** A revolt against a government but less organized than a revolution.

The U.S. Ground War in Vietnam 1965–1973

and other vital bases by U.S. combat troops, and it was the arrival of these troops which effectively signaled the start of the USA's involvement, on an escalating basis, in the ground war in South Vietnam.

The USA had already begun to strengthen the defense of Da Nang early in February, when a US Marine Corps air-defense battalion arrived with its complement of HAWK surface-to-air missiles, launchers, and associated equipment. Late in the same month, Westmoreland's deputy, Lieutenant General John Throckmorton, visited Da Nang and soon reported the tactical situation to be so dangerous that a complete Marine expeditionary brigade (three infantry battalions with artillery and logistical support) was required as a matter of urgency. Westmoreland trimmed the recommendation from three to two battalions, and recommended such a deployment.

Vietnamese force, which was low in morale and unwilling to undertake all but the most limited patrol work. Da Nang was a base from which many of the Rolling Thunder attacks were launched, and could thus only be a magnet for Communist attack. The only realistic solution, if many millions of dollars-worth of aircraft and other matériel were not to be lost, was the replacement of the South Vietnamese troops around Da Nang

OPPOSITE: Sfc. Willie C. Smith, 1st Special Forces Group, Nui Ba Den, is shown teaching grenade practice to Vietnamese volunteers.

ABOVE: Three North American T-28s escort a Lockheed Hercules transporting munitions over Vietnam.

RIGHT: A Viet Cong prisoner, recently taken captive.

Maxwell Taylor was concerned that the deployment would open the conceptual floodgates to an ever-increasing flow of U.S. combat troops to South Vietnam, and a parallel South Vietnamese abandonment of as much combat as possible to the Americans, but nonetheless felt that Westmoreland was right and added his support to the request sent to Washington, which gained further recommendation from Admiral Ulysses S. Grant Sharp, the commander in chief Pacific. President Johnson authorized such a deployment on February 26, and on March 8 Brigadier General Frederick J. Karsh's 9th Marine Expeditionary Brigade landed on the beach at Da Nang. These were not in fact the first men of the U.S. Marine Corps to see service in South Vietnam, this honor going to Marine advisers who had served with the Vietnamese Marines since 1954, and the Marines' "Shu-Fly" helicopter task unit which had been operational at Da Nang since 1962. Even so, the advent of the 9th Marine Expeditionary Brigade was a momentous step in the development of the Vietnam War.

As the 9th Marine Expeditionary Brigade, which was soon redesignated as the III Marine Amphibious Force, began to arrive, Westmoreland perceived the South Vietnamese military situation as critical, as noted above. He believed that the situation

ABOVE: An officer examines the entrance to a NLF bunker complex. The Communist forces were notably adept at constructing and using such complexes in many parts of South Vietnam.

OPPOSITE LEFT: General William Westmoreland.

OPPOSITE: Four of seven prisoners captured in a Viet Cong tunnel complex in the Thanh Dien Forest during Operation Cedar Falls. During the course of the campaign, U.S. infantrymen discovered and destroyed a massive tunnel complex in the Iron Triangle, used as the headquarters for guerrilla raids and terrorist attacks on Saigon.

The U.S. Ground War in Vietnam 1965–1973

in six months, unless there was a momentous change, would become one in which the South Vietnamese would hold only "a series of islands of strength clustered around district and province capitals," the South Vietnamese administration crippled by internal dissent between various factions advocating different levels of accord with the Communists. Westmoreland's gloomy prognostication was based on the current situation, but further gravity was added by the fact that the MACV commander knew that a division of the North Vietnamese army had infiltrated its way into secure positions in the mountains and jungles of South Vietnam's Central Highlands. This was clearly only the vanguard of larger North Vietnamese army forces committed to operations in South Vietnam, but Westmoreland had no idea how large a force the North Vietnamese intended to deploy into South Vietnam. In fact, the North Vietnamese intended to commit very sizeable forces to implement a 1964 decision of the North Vietnamese administration to force a military decision in South Vietnam before U.S. forces could be committed in large

15

The Fatal Commitment

numbers. Even with the limited intelligence information available to him early in 1965, Westmoreland knew that the North Vietnamese deployment into the Central Highlands marked the beginning of the change from an internal war of **insurgency** in South Vietnam, with North Vietnamese support, to a conventional war based in increasing measure on the commitment of significant North Vietnamese regular forces.

It would need something in the order of a year, even if the necessary change of attitude and commitment could be imposed on the South Vietnamese, to raise their army to the level of capability at which it could handle the increasing activity of the Viet Cong insurgents, and the presence of North Vietnamese regular forces was not factored into this assessment. Even if U.S. bombing led the North Vietnamese to the negotiating table, which he believed to be a forlorn hope, Westmoreland believed that it would happen only at the end of a six-month aerial effort, by which time the South Vietnamese defense might well have dissolved.

Westmoreland believed the optimum solution to the problem, as it now existed, was the creation of an international force of about five divisions. This would be delivered by sea to points along the **DMZ** and by air and land across the Laotian panhandle, which was the region of Laos through which the Ho Chi Minh Trail extended to the west and south

LEFT: A U.S. Marine outside a burning Vietnamese house.

OPPOSITE: Corporal Lindy R. Hall of 3rd Platoon, K Company, 3rd Battalion, 3rd Marines, sets fire to a Vietnamese hut during Operation Prairie III in 1967.

of Vietnam above and below the DMZ. Such a force would offer significant military strength in its own right, and by its very creation serve to advise the North Vietnamese that the Western world would not tolerate Communist aggression against South Vietnam. Even if Johnson had approved the idea, which he did not, it would still have taken several months to create and deploy such a force. In the circumstances, therefore, Westmoreland had no option but to call for the deployment of more U.S. combat rather than support troops to hold the Communist forces in check until such time as the South Vietnamese army had been turned into an effective force.

The North Vietnamese division's deployment into the Central Highlands suggested that the Communist plan was to sever South Vietnam though its narrowest point, before striking north to take the northern portion of the divided country. It made sense to Westmoreland, therefore, to deploy a U.S. division into this high-threat area, and to receive two more U.S. Marine Corps battalions to guard the air bases in the threatened northern provinces, so that they could continue to function effectively within the context of the Rolling Thunder campaign.

5 Scariest Booby Traps of the Vietnam War

The proposals were recommended to Johnson when Taylor visited Washington late in March, but the U.S. ambassador immediately discovered that the president was still vacillating about the advisability of an enlarged U.S. commitment to South Vietnam. Johnson therefore approved the deployment only of two U.S. Marine Corps battalions for the air base protection task. Even so, Taylor was able to convince Johnson to agree to a so-called "enclave strategy," which seemed to Westmoreland to be wrong. This strategy was based on the creation of defensive enclaves centered on air bases and ports in a process that was economical in terms of troop requirements, but nonetheless confirmed the USA's determination to support South Vietnam. In another significant change to the "rules of engagement" pertinent to South Vietnam, Johnson conceded that the U.S. could abandon the previously mandated defensive posture and patrol to a radius of 50 miles (80 km) from any enclave, with the object of disrupting any Communist build-up and preparations for an attack on the enclave in question.

The trouble with Johnson's decisions was that while the number of men who might have to be deployed was kept to the minimum, they offered protection only to U.S. interests, and at the same time revealed a diplomatically significant indecision of longer-term strategic purpose. This became all the more evident when Johnson summoned a conference of senior figures of the administration and the military. Those involved, apart from Johnson himself, included McNamara, Taylor, Westmoreland, and General Earle G. Wheeler, chairman of the Joint Chiefs of Staff, the conference assembling at Honolulu on April 20. Here there was not a single expression of confidence

The Fatal Commitment

in the successful outcome of the Rolling Thunder campaign without a parallel improvement of the situation on the ground in South Vietnam. All agreed that the only way in which this improvement could be secured was the commitment of a further nine battalions of U.S. troops, so raising the total in South Vietnam to 13 battalions, and at the same time beginning the start of an undertaking to create an international force, as first suggested in recent times by Westmoreland, from other South-East Asian, East Asian, and Australasian countries, most especially Australia, New Zealand, and South Korea.

The decision to solicit the support of other countries, otherwise the "More Flags" policy, in fact had its origins in 1961, when a number of administration officials had recommended the creation and deployment of a 25,000-man force taken from the members of the SEATO alliance, including the USA, UK, Australia, France, New Zealand,

OPPOSITE: U.S. Army personnel in the Rung Sat Special Zone.

RIGHT: The U.S. Navy Cimarron-class fleet oiler USS *Guadalupe* (AO-32) refueling the Australian guided missile destroyer HMAS *Hobart* (D39) in the spring of 1967. HMAS *Hobart* was taking part in Operation "Sea Dragon." "Sea Dragon" was a series of naval operations beginning in 1966 to interdict sea lines of communications and supplies going south from North Vietnam to South Vietnam, and to destroy land targets with naval gunfire. The primary purpose of Sea Dragon forces was the interception and destruction of water borne logistic craft (WBLC), which ranged in size from large self propelled barges down to small junks and sampans.

the Philippines, Thailand and, at that time, Pakistan. It was recommended that such a force be deployed either on the border between Laos and South Vietnam or in the Central Highlands. The UK, France, and Pakistan expressed themselves unwilling to contribute, the first to respond positively being Australia, which sent 30 jungle warfare experts to reinforce the U.S. advisory teams in the northern provinces of South Vietnam during August 1962. By 1969, more than 7,000 Australians were serving in Vietnam, along with about 550 New Zealand troops, as the manpower of three combat battalions and five air squadrons (one bomber, one helicopter, and three transport). Another element of Australian support was the Royal Australian Navy's destroyer *Perth*, later relieved by her sister, *Hobart*, which operated with elements of the U.S. Navy.

Eventually five other nations provided troops for the anti-Communist effort in South Vietnam. Other than Australia and New Zealand, these were the Philippines, South Korea, and Thailand, and there were miniscule parties of less than 30 men each from Spain and Taiwan. The non-U.S. contribution to the war effort in South Vietnam reached its peak in 1969, as 68,900 combat troops and 34 other countries provided support of a non-combatant nature. The arrival of these other "foreign" troops presented a problem of command: while the U.S. population would never have stood for the commitment of U.S. troops under South Vietnamese command, the South Vietnamese were unwilling to commit themselves, for reasons of obvious national pride, to service under U.S. command. While a unified command structure would have offered the standard military advantages, Westmoreland did not want to press for such an arrangement for political and diplomatic reasons: the commitment of South Vietnamese troops under U.S. command would have played into the hands of the North Vietnamese, who claimed that the South Vietnamese were already "puppets" of the Americans, and might also have set back the U.S. efforts to persuade the South

The Fatal Commitment

Vietnamese to play a more effective and self-reliant role in the war by reforming their armed forces. In this respect Westmoreland was fully in accord with the USA's perception that the war in South Vietnam could be won, at the military as well as the political level, only by the South Vietnamese, with the Americans providing support.

Westmoreland therefore opted for a dual-command system, more fully integrated, it was hoped, by close co-ordination at all command levels. Within "foreign" forces also maintained their own identities, but were also involved in the program of close coordination. It was a flexible system which could have paved the way for the emergence of inter-allied rivalries, but in South Vietnam the arrangement appears to have worked with little problem.

Within the U.S. chain of command, Westmoreland's headquarters remained in essentially the same position that the MACV had occupied since its creation in February 1962. The MACV was thus a joint command, including elements of all four U.S. forces, but with the U.S. Army predominant, and was subordinate to the commander in chief Pacific, Admiral Sharp, headquartered in the Hawaiian Islands with responsibility for the entire Pacific region. Westmoreland had responsibility for all operations inside South Vietnam and also for tactical air attacks in Laos and the southern part of North Vietnam just above the DMZ, while Sharp exercised responsibility for air operations over the rest of North Vietnam. Also under Sharp's overall command was the 7th

RIGHT: Viet Cong suspects by the Mekong river.

The U.S. Ground War in Vietnam 1965–1973

The Fatal Commitment

AUSTRALIA'S INVOLVEMENT IN THE VIETNAM WAR

Australia's involvement in the Vietnam War began with the arrival of a small commitment of military advisers (The Australian Army Training Team Vietnam (AATTV) during July and August 1962. Australia's support for South Vietnam was on the request of Ngo Dinh Diem, South Vietnam's leader and was in keeping with the policies of other nations at the time. This was driven by the rise of communisim in south-east Asia after the second world war.

As the war escalated, the Australian government increased troop numbers by calling up conscripts under the National Service Scheme in place at the time. By the time the Vietnam War ended Australia had witnessed its longest conflict so far in the 20th century. In the early years of the war, Australia's involvement was not widely opposed by the Australian pubic, but as troop numbers grew to a battalion in 1965 and finally a task force in 1966, the public became increasingly concerned about the war. By the time Australia's military withdrew from Vietnam, approximately 60,000 Australian servicemen had served. Involvement in the war cost 521 Australian lives, while some 3,000 servicemen were injured or became ill. The Australian military finally commenced withdrawl from Vietnam in November 1970. This was as a consequence of the strategy of "Vietnamization" which handed back military action to South Vietnam's own forces. In the aftermath of the Vietnam War, Australia adopted a more independent foreign policy.

Fleet, although Westmoreland was able to call on this for tactical air attacks on targets in South Vietnam by carrier-borne warplanes. At a later stage, after the use of the B-52 Stratofortress heavy bomber over Vietnam had been authorized, overall command was exercised from the USA by the commander in chief Strategic Air Command, although the headquarters of the MACV was responsible for the recommendation of targets for approval in Washington. Though not formally required, it gradually developed that all signals between Westmoreland and Sharp were copied to the Joint Chiefs of Staff.

With the growth of the U.S. military strength in South Vietnam, it became necessary to establish subordinate commands for the U.S. Army, USAF, and U.S. Navy/U.S. Marine Corps components as the U.S. Army, Vietnam as an administrative and logistical command, the 7th Air Force, and the Naval Force, Vietnam. By this time the South Vietnamese had already divided their nation into four "corps tactical zones," and in three of these the U.S. created parallel American commands along the lines of a corps headquarters. The I Corps zone covered the northern provinces, and in this the U.S. headquarters was the III Marine Amphibious Force. The II Corps zone covered the central provinces, and in this the U.S. headquarters was the I Field Force. And the III Corps zone comprised the provinces centered on Saigon, and in this the U.S. headquarters was the II Field Force. The last South Vietnamese corps tactical zone was the IV Corps area, comprising the provinces of the Mekong river delta and here, where large U.S. forces were to be committed, command of the U.S. forces was allocated to the senior U.S. adviser to the commander of the South Vietnamese IV Corps. The senior adviser role in the other corps zones fell to the commanders of the I Field Force, II Field Force, and III Marine Amphibious Force.

As the nine battalions approved by the administration began to reach South Vietnam in May and June 1975, Johnson tacitly forgot the "enclave strategy" when he permitted Westmoreland to engage in "counter-insurgency combat operations." The administration was worried that the U.S. public would perceive these changes as an enlargement of the U.S. commitment to South Vietnam, however, and therefore did not publicly reveal the widening of Westmoreland's remit. Thus there began "head in the sand" perception

ABOVE: HMAS *Perth* (D38) fires on North Vietnamese coastal defense sites in February 1968.

that the U.S. public could readily be fooled, for U.S. journalists in South Vietnam rapidly appreciated and also reported that U.S. forces were not merely holding defensive positions around key bases and the like, but starting to take the war actively to the Communist forces. Despite this, the administration continued to maintain that there had been no change in the U.S. forces' "defensive mission": thus was created the credibility gap between the Johnson administration and the media, and by extension between the administration and the public, which was destined to play a significant part in the conduct and thus the outcome of the Vietnam War.

The move of new U.S. units and formations into South Vietnam was comparatively slow, and had to be followed by a period of acclimatization in both the climatic and tactical senses.

So it was some time before the new forces could start to play any major role in the conduct of the ground war in South Vietnam. The Communists did not waste the opportunity presented to them, and the Viet Cong thus stepped up the tempo of its recruitment efforts and increased the number and strength of its attacks. Operating at up to regimental strength, the Communist forces captured some district capitals, ambushed and destroyed one South Vietnamese battalion, and besieged an outpost in the Central Highlands. Events of this type and nature themselves suggested the imminence of a major crisis, but the South Vietnamese position was saved, at least temporarily, by the unexpectedly lethargic performance of the North Vietnamese division in the Central Highlands.

This presented Johnson with the opportunity to implement a number of other measures, including the dispatch of several U.S. Coast Guard vessels to support the fledgling South Vietnamese navy in its immensely difficult task of seeking to halt the flow of Communist reinforcements into South Vietnam by sea. Johnson issued permission for the 7th Fleet to provide air and gunfire support for U.S. Marine Corps operating in the northern provinces. But perhaps of

Remembering Vietnam: 40 years from Australia's withdrawal

The Fatal Commitment

the greatest importance of all, Johnson responded favorably to a request from Westmoreland for the use of B-52 heavy bombers, initially from the U.S. bases on Guam in the Marianas Islands group but later from bases in Thailand, in attacks on the Communist forces' bases in jungle and mountain regions too remote for any land attack to be practical. These bases were so well dug-in and protected that attacks by tactical warplanes had provided no success worthy of the name, but the B-52 bombers, operating at very high altitude where they could be neither heard nor seen from the ground, were able to bomb accurately and devastate the whole of a base area with a massive weight of free-fall ordnance. With total destruction visited on them by aircraft they did not even know to be in the area, the Communist forces came to dread the B-52 more than any other single weapon used in the Vietnam War.

These moves were individually useful, but could not check, let alone reverse, a military situation which was becoming ever more parlous. The crisis in the land war perhaps inevitably resulted in another change

ABOVE: A South Vietnamese army interpreter questions a Viet Cong prisoner before passing his answers on to Capt. Dennis K. Anderson in September 1967, during Operation Cook. This was a search-and-destroy mission being conducted in the mountains of Quang Ngai province, approximately 320 miles (515km) north-east of Saigon, by elements of the 2nd Battalion, 502nd Infantry, 101st Airborne Brigade.

in the government of South Vietnam. There had been a weak attempt at a coup d'état in May, and in its aftermath Quat attempted to revise his cabinet. He failed in this attempt, resigned, and handed the government over to the military, which was, of course, already the de facto ruler of the country. With the South Vietnamese air force to the fore, the military established a ten-man Committee for the Direction of the State with General Nguyen Cao Ky as prime minister and General Nguyen Van Thieu as head of state. Given the nature of South Vietnamese politics up to this time, there was every reason to suppose that the new administration would not last long, but the doubters were, in fact, to be proved wrong.

Given the apparently volatile nature of the South Vietnamese administration and the effective disintegration of the South Vietnamese Army, which was losing battalions more rapidly than replacement units could be raised and trained, the collapse of South Vietnam seemed imminent. Westmoreland came to the inevitable conclusion that the situation could be stabilized only by a major injection of new U.S. combat troops. At this time, it had become clear, the Communists' major units had adopted the tactics of decoying South Vietnamese units deep into sparsely populated areas for destruction or such decimation that they ceased to be effective. This left the more heavily populated areas with little or no defense, which were then easy prey to the local Communist guerrilla forces in the areas around cities and towns, and for the political cadres within the cities and towns. This two-handed approach was therefore destroying the South Vietnamese army and leaving the urban areas prey to terrorism, intimidation, and the assassination of professional men, such as doctors, teachers, lawyers, and administrators. The only solution was to deploy more U.S. combat troops to assume the main burden of fighting the Communists' larger units, so leaving the South Vietnamese army free to protect the population of the urban areas.

So Westmoreland requested the forces to boost the U.S. presence in South Vietnam to 34 battalions, with ten from other countries: this was, admittedly, not a force large enough to win the war, but just enough to prevent a South Vietnamese defeat. Westmoreland's request provoked considerable controversy in Washington and, as the arguments continued, Johnson gave Westmoreland the authorization to

BELOW: An M48 tank in action in 1969. Some of these were assigned to U.S. Marine Corps units, arriving in Vietnam in 1965, while others went to three U.S. Army battalions, the 1/77th Armor near the DMZ, the 1/69th Armor in the Central Highlands, and the 2/34th Armor near the Mekong delta.

make use of U.S. troops in any situation in which Westmoreland thought it necessary "to strengthen the relative position" of the South Vietnamese. The wording was clearly ambiguous, but Westmoreland took it as permission to justify the launch of

The Fatal Commitment

the first large-scale U.S. operation of the war, namely a raid into War Zone D, a long-established Communist sanctuary to the north-west of Saigon and in the area which also included the U.S. air base at Bien Hoa.

Centered on the U.S. 173rd Airborne Brigade, a force of U.S., Australian/New Zealand and South Vietnamese troops, totaling eight battalions, force struck into the sanctuary on June 27. There were several sharp clashes but, like most raids, the operation was inconclusive, although there are some indications that it threw the Communist forces temporarily off balance, thus preventing a planned attack on Bien Hoa. The Australian troops were of the 1st Battalion, Royal Australian Regiment, and were part of a 1,400-strong Australian force which had arrived in South Vietnam only recently. The force was limited by its current Australian remit to "local security operations" within a radius of 22 miles (35km) from Bien Hoa; in fact the Australian soldiers were undertaking search-and-destroy patrols in conjunction with U.S. forces within days of their arrival. A New Zealand artillery unit, arriving at the same time as the main Australian force, was committed equally quickly.

Still uncertain about his response to Westmoreland's request for additional "fact-finding mission" to Saigon with McNamara and Henry Cabot Lodge, earlier the U.S. ambassador to South Vietnam and

ABOVE: Marines from the USMC Combined Action Platoon Oscar-3, entering Tum Piang Ville.

OPPOSITE: A USAF H-34 helicopter operating in Vietnam.

soon to return in this position as Taylor's successor, at its head. Westmoreland told McNamara that it would need about 175,000 U.S. troops merely to stabilize the position in South Vietnam, with another 100,000 following to ensure that the situation was kept under control and then turned to advantage. Westmoreland added that he could "halt the losing trend" with this troop strength by the end of 1965, undertake a long offensive in 1966 and, in the aftermath of that successful first effort, defeat, or capture the surviving Communist forces over a period of 12 to 18 months.

When the fact-finding team reported back to Washington, there was still determined opposition from officials who saw the dangers inherent in an open-ended commitment of this size to any larger-scale U.S. involvement in South Vietnam. But both McNamara and the Joint Chiefs-of-Staff supported Westmoreland, and Johnson acceded to the request. On July 28 the president appeared on national television to state: "I have today ordered to Vietnam the Airmobile Division [1st Cavalry Division (Airmobile), only recently formed] and certain other forces which will raise our fighting strength from 75,000 to 125,000 men almost immediately. Additional forces will be needed later, and they will be sent as requested."

This announcement marked a turning point in the Vietnam War, as the USA had thereby committed itself to a war which was to prove altogether more bloody, costly, difficult, and lengthy than anyone in the USA had yet conceived. It would be only after seven years, and with the war still not concluded, that a morally divided USA would be able to extricate itself after suffering extremely high losses.

As he received news of Johnson's authorization for the dispatch of the forces he needed, Westmoreland saw the situation in South Vietnam as akin to a building (the South Vietnamese state and people) whose foundations were being eaten away and weakened by termites (Communist cadres and irregular forces), so that when the foundations had been sufficiently weakened the building could be toppled by the advent of other destructive elements (the major units of the Communist forces lurking in the jungles and mountains). Westmoreland felt that the first step in defeating this infestation was to destroy the major units, or at least to harass them so severely that they would be incapable of attacking the building, thereby providing the breathing time in which the irregular forces and cadres could be

The Fatal Commitment

destroyed systematically and the building repaired.

Thus Westmoreland decided right from the start to use his U.S. combat forces to fight the Communists' major units, leaving the protection of the South Vietnamese population, the defeat of the irregulars, and the elimination of the cadres to the South Vietnamese army; the all-important task of improving the civil population's way of life would be left to the South Vietnamese administration with the support of U.S. civilian agencies. This broad concept fell into three phases. The first involved the use of American troops to protect the development of the logistical bases which were essential, given South Vietnam's underdeveloped infrastructure and lack of vital military facilities, such as airfields, ports, storage facilities, and communications networks. Westmoreland envisaged, nonetheless, that even during this essentially preparatory stage and an immediate threat by Communist major forces, some units could be diverted to check them. The second phase involved a drive into South Vietnam's sparsely populated hinterlands to reach and destroy the Communist bases, a process which would bring the Communist forces to battle in fighting favorable to the U.S. forces' superior firepower on land and in the air. The third phase was based on the implementation of sustained offensive operations against the Communists' major units, with the object of destroying or crippling them sufficiently for the strengthened South Vietnamese army to complete the process of their elimination with only limited U.S. support.

The primary reasons for Westmoreland's decision to rely on U.S. rather than South Vietnamese troops to take on the Communist enemy's major units was first their possession of greater firepower and mobility, second their ability to bring that firepower to bear usefully in remote regions, thus reducing the probability of catastrophic casualties and physical damage in more densely populated regions, and third the probability that South Vietnamese troops would not fight with any notable dedication against members of the same ethnic group when dealing with their own people. Despite the second reason above, Westmoreland had decided that whenever they were not needed in the remoter areas, U.S. troops would be deployed for operations against less capable Communist units in the more densely populated parts of South Vietnam.

As suggested above, it had been the U.S. intention right from the start that military operations would be only one part of the overall U.S. effort, whose other aspect was a series of civic action programs to improve the everyday lives of the people of South Vietnam. This was not a wholly altruistic factor but an intrinsic element of a "hearts and mind" undertaking designed to boost the South Vietnamese population's adherence to its government. Westmoreland appreciated that once they had discovered the basic tenets of the U.S. effort, they might attempt to keep the major U.S. forces engaged in remoter areas and therefore not in any position to aid the South Vietnamese civil population, but felt that the greater mobility of his forces would make it all but impossible for the Communists' major forces to keep the U.S. forces committed in remoter areas for any extended period. Even if the Communists did succeed in this,

RIGHT: The Chinook helicopter played an important part in the movement of equipment and troops.

The U.S. Ground War in Vietnam 1965–1973

The Fatal Commitment

moreover, this too would serve a purpose inasmuch as the Communist forces could not then become involved in attacks on the main centres of urban population.

Another factor Westmoreland was forced to contend with was the security of South Vietnam's 900-mile (1450-km) frontier. It was clearly impossible to seal the full length of this tightly enough to prevent infiltration, and the only alternative was reliance on fixed frontier posts around which the infiltrators would have to pass patrols and aerial reconnaissance to find and locate the forces which were infiltrating through gaps between the frontier posts and, finally, artillery, air attack, and mobile ground forces to fix and destroy any groups discovered.

The key to protecting the frontier positions was to employ men from the ethnic minority populations, aided by advisers from the U.S. Army's special forces, for the men of these remoter regions knew their own territory intimately, often had little love for the Vietnamese, and were skillful and fearsome fighters. As far as the notoriously porous DMZ was concerned, Westmoreland still hoped that an international "peacekeeping" force might be made available to seal this sector of the frontier.

The most difficult problem facing the U.S. and South Vietnamese forces, however, was the network of extemporized roads, tracks, and paths collectively known as the Ho Chi Minh Trail. Passing from North Vietnam into neutral Laos and Cambodia, it offered the Communists a veritable mass of avenues along which to pass men, matériel, and supplies that were virtually undetectable, except in miniscule portions, was impossible to sever, being possessed of so many tentacles, and lay largely in neutral countries. Westmoreland did hope eventually to sever and close the Ho Chi Minh Trail through Laos and northern Cambodia, but did not initially request authority to enter Laos as he felt that the forces on hand were too small to allow any diversion of strength for the task.

What it all amounted to was, in effect, a war of attrition, because there was no single enemy formation against which Westmoreland could direct the U.S. strength for a decisive campaign of the type forming the heart of the U.S. military philosophy. He was faced with political restrictions denying him the right to undertake military operations outside South Vietnam, and the prospect of a force sufficient to hold only portions of South Vietnam in any strength, so Westmoreland could envisage no alternative.

This meant the Vietnam War would inevitably be long, as are all wars of attrition, but there was the longer-term prospect that an American success and a revitalized South Vietnam would create a security situation in which the Viet Cong would be unable to recruit or impress sufficient South Vietnamese to maintain their struggle. This would

OPPOSITE: Two suspected members of the Viet Cong are loaded aboard a jeep by members of the U.S. 173rd Airborne Brigade, while conducting a two-day airmobile tactical exercise in Vietnam in May 1965.

ABOVE: A CH-47A Chinook brings the main body of 3rd Brigade troops down on to the mountain ridge of secured Landing Zone 5.

leave the North Vietnamese with regular units with which to continue the war on their own against strengthening anti-Communist forces, that would ultimately result in insupportable losses.

The general scheme was that U.S. divisions and brigades should be located at semi-permanent base camps and operate from these into the surrounding region that would constitute the division's or brigade's area of tactical responsibility; there was also provision for the division or brigade to be moved, on a temporary basis, to tackle major Communist formations and units in other parts of South Vietnam. In such an eventuality, the division or brigade would detach a small security force which would be left to garrison the base camp. The rest of the division or brigade would move out into the required area and there construct a temporary base camp shielded, at a distance, by fire-support bases prepared for all-round defense and operating as artillery firing positions and patrol bases. Depending on intelligence assessments of the opposition's strength, components of the division or brigade, up to a strength of several battalions, would be launched on sweeps of the region around the fire-support bases, bringing the Communist forces to combat in conditions where the U.S. firepower superiority, especially in artillery, would be dominant. In overall terms, this was the system known as "search-and-destroy."

Even though U.S. firepower was to be concentrated in the remoter regions of South Vietnam, it was conceded that damage to villages was inevitable. On occasions, the Communist forces might be so deeply entrenched within villages and among

The Fatal Commitment

ABOVE: Helicopters were used in the Bong Son district during the search-and-destroy mission, Operation White Wing, to move personnel of the 1st Cavalry Division (Airmobile) into the assault area in search of the Viet Cong.

LEFT: U.S. Skyraiders fall into position for an air strike against Viet Cong bases in South Vietnam. The aircraft, which carried bombs, napalm, and 20-mm cannons, were flown by Vietnamese pilots accompanied by American advisers.

OPPOSITE: Troops crossing paddyfields in 1968.

The U.S. Ground War in Vietnam 1965–1973

the civilian population that relocation of the civilians would have to be undertaken and their original settlement destroyed to create "free-fire zones" in which the Communist forces could be found, fixed, and destroyed, opening the possibility that the original inhabitants might be able to return at a later date. Neither of the only alternatives to this tactical scheme, either to enter combat with the civil population still present, or to abandon the area to the Communists, was acceptable for fear of causing high civilian casualties and because, if left to their own devices, the Communists would be able to extend the area and depth of their control over the region and civil population.

Text-Dependent Questions

1. Why was the airbase at Da Nang a magnet for Communist attack?

2. How many other countries became involved in the Vietnam War?

3. What was the Ho Chi Minh trail?

Research Projects

Summarize General Westmoreland's strategic objectives during the Vietnam War.

Chapter Two
AMERICA'S FIRST MAJOR OFFENSIVE

The first major offensive operation involving only U.S. troops took place in August 1965, when U.S. Marines, protecting an airfield on the north-central coast at Chu Lai, located a Viet Cong regiment on the Van Tuong peninsula. Since the Viet Cong force was a mere 15 miles (24km) distant, and was therefore a tactical threat to Chu Lai, the commander of the III Marine Amphibious Force, Lieutenant General Lewis W. Walt, inaugurated Operation Starlite. This was launched on the basis of intelligence information provided by Major General Nguyen Chanh Thi, the commander of the South Vietnamese forces in I Corps area in northern South Vietnam.

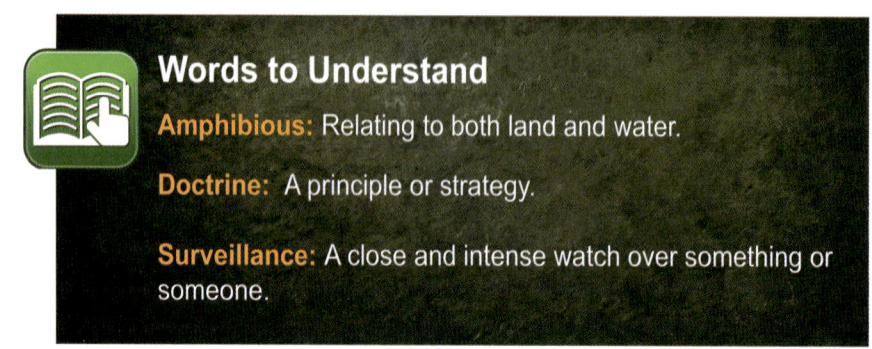

The operation was undertaken as a combined arms undertaking, involving ground, air, and naval units, the core of the effort being the deployment of men of the U.S. Marine Corps by helicopter into the designated landing zone, while more men of the same corps were delivered by **amphibious** landing. The operation began on August 17, 1965, and

Words to Understand

Amphibious: Relating to both land and water.

Doctrine: A principle or strategy.

Surveillance: A close and intense watch over something or someone.

The U.S. Ground War in Vietnam 1965–1973

OPPOSITE: U.S. soldiers with a Viet Cong prisoner.

RIGHT: Robert Strange McNamara was an American business executive and the eighth Secretary of Defense, serving from 1961 to 1968 under Presidents John F. Kennedy and Lyndon B. Johnson, during which time he played a major role in escalating the United States involvement in the Vietnam War.

BELOW RIGHT: Tank landing ship USS *Vernon County*.

BELOW: Lieutenent General Lewis William Walt.

involved 5,500 men of the 9th Marine Amphibious Brigade. The brigade comprised the 2nd Battalion 4th Marines (2/4), 3rd Battalion 3rd Marines (3/3), 3rd Battalion 7th Marines (3/7), and 3rd Battalion 7th Marines (3/7) from the Special Landing Force (originally a reserve component). Also involved were the U.S. Navy's cruiser *Galveston* and dock landing ship *Cabildo* for naval gunfire support, the 3rd Battalion 12th Marines being the artillery unit in direct support. The tank landing ship *Vernon County* carried elements of the 3rd Battalion 3rd Marines at Chu Lai, and steamed south along the coast to An Thuong, where the men were landed.

The Viet Cong forces, totaling some 1,500 men, comprised the 1st Viet Cong Regiment, made up of the 60th and 80th Viet Cong Battalions, the 52nd Viet Cong Company, and one company of the 45th Viet Cong Weapons Battalion.

"Mike" Company of 3/3 was to be the blocking force for deployment on August 17, using tracked landing

America's First Major Offensive

The U.S. Ground War in Vietnam 1965–1973

OPPOSITE: Defoliation Mission. A UH-1D helicopter from the 336th Aviation Company sprays a defoliation agent (Agent Orange) on agricultural land in the Mekong delta to destroy cover.

ABOVE: Sergeant Curtis E. Hester firing his M-16 rifle, Sergeant Billy H. Faulks calls for air support, Co D, 151st (Ranger) Infantry, Vietnam War, 1969.

vehicles to reach its landing area; after coming ashore the men were to move 4 miles (6.4 km) to establish the required block. The 3rd Battalion 3rd Marines was then to make its amphibious landing and begin to drive the Viet Cong towards 2/4, which was to be lifted by helicopter into three landing zones west of Van Tuong. Secrecy was paramount, and no South Vietnamese army commander or units were to be informed of the forthcoming operation.

The men of the U.S. Marine Corps met only light resistance as they moved in to the attack. "Echo" Company, 2/4, spotted Viet Cong in the open and called in artillery fire from the 3rd Battalion 12th Marines, a barrage which is said to have killed 90 Viet Cong soldiers. "Hotel" Company, 2/4, then assaulted the 60th Viet Cong Battalion, which resisted strongly. One prisoner was taken and 40 weapons were captured. "India" Company, 3/3, attacked An Cuong after taking heavy fire from the hamlet and losing its company commander in the engagement.

"India" Company was ordered to join "Kilo" and "Hotel" Companies

37

America's First Major Offensive

and clean up any opposition, but was caught in a cross fire from Nam Yen Dan Hill 30. "Hotel" Company established a defensive perimeter and was then instructed to wait for reinforcements, but this additional strength was diverted to assist the supply column which had been ambushed west of its position. Recoilless rifle fire from the Viet Cong positions hit five tracked landing vehicles and three flamethrower tanks, and the men of the U.S. Marine Corps had to mount a rescue, suffering five dead and 17 wounded after they were hit by heavy mortar and rifle fire. The Marines called in artillery and air support to suppress the mortar and automatic fire.

The evolving nature of the engagement required the deployment of "Lima" Company, 3/7, from the helicopter assault carrier *Iwo Jima* to join "India" Company in providing assistance to the ambushed supply column. Toward nightfall, the Marines settled into defensive positions. The other Marines of the 3/7 landed during the night, and the battalion prepared itself for a morning assault on the Viet Cong positions; when it attacked, however, it discovered that the Viet Cong had decamped in the night, moving off into the mountainous area inland of the peninsula. There was still resistance from other Viet Cong pockets of resistance in bunkers and caves, but this had been overcome by the end of the day.

The Marine units reported killing 614 Viet Cong soldiers, and other American gains were nine prisoners, 42 suspected guerrillas, and 109 weapons. The 1st Viet Cong Regiment, however, had not been totally destroyed as the Marines had hoped. The Marines reported the loss of 45 dead and 203 wounded, while other sources claim the U.S. losses were 54, in the form of 52 Marines, one U.S. Navy corpsman, and one U.S. Army major flying gunship support.

Lessons learned from the battle by the U.S. forces included the knowledge that the daily allotment of two gallons of water per man was inadequate in the heat of Vietnam, and that the M14 rifle was too bulky for troops cramped into small personnel carriers. Starlite was a major psychological boost for the U.S. forces, having for the first time engaged in a main-force Viet Cong unit and emerged victorious. As was to be the pattern repeated in many an operation to follow, however, the men of the U.S. Marine Corps were too few in number to garrison the peninsula, and the inevitable result was that in the years of fighting still to come the Communist forces would return and the operation would have to be repeated from time to time.

Meanwhile, the threat that the North Vietnamese division in the Central Highlands would drive to the sea and split South Vietnam in two parts had been slowly developing. During October 1965 some 6,000 North Vietnamese troops began to concentrate against a South Vietnamese outpost near the border at Plei Me, as the first step in eliminating three outposts in the region, taking the provincial capital of Pleiku and advancing along Highway 19 to the sea.

ABOVE: A USAF A-1E Skyraider releases 500-lb bombs over a Viet Cong target in South Vietnam in April 1965.

OPPOSITE ABOVE: The M42A1 Duster was an improvement on the old M19 twin 40-mm antiaircraft tank of the Second World War, and was engaged in much action throughout the Vietman conflict.

OPPOSITE BELOW: A U.S. Navy Patrol Air Cushion Vehicle (PACV) hovercraft picking up Viet Cong personnel.

The U.S. Ground War in Vietnam 1965–1973

When the U.S. 1st Cavalry Division (Airmobile) arrived on Highway 19 at An Khe, where a base camp was quickly created, Westmoreland planned to commit at least part of the freshly arrived formation against the continuing North Vietnamese build-up. Although the South Vietnamese, with U.S. air support, were able to break the Communist encirclement of the outpost at Plei Me, a Communist concentration was reported still to be operating in the area, namely in the dense jungle of the Ia Drang valley.

The resulting campaign can be seen as a microcosm of the Vietnam War in terms of its planning, execution, and tactics, and is therefore worthy of consideration in detail. The major lesson drawn from the U.S. Army's experiences in the Korean War

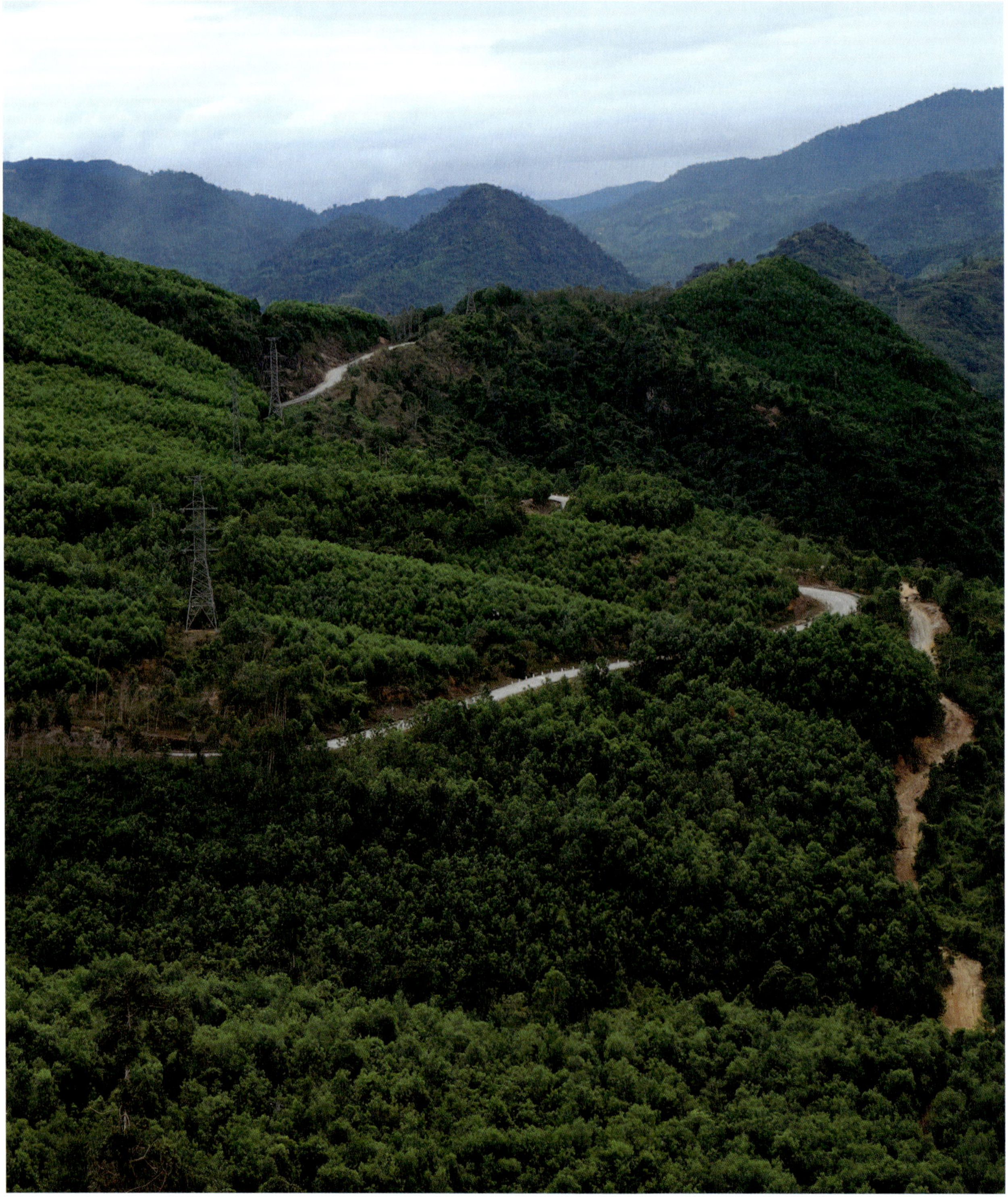

The U.S. Ground War in Vietnam 1965–1973

was the need to overcome the limitations imposed by terrain, and this was something which only airborne troops and aircraft could achieve. The famous airborne divisions of the U.S. Army emerged from the Korean War with their reputations intact and the Airborne School at Fort Benning, Georgia, continued to train generations of a junior leadership elite. The U.S. Army was not as fortunate with its aircraft, and in 1952 decided to raise 12 battalions of helicopters to carry

OPPOSITE: A modern view of part of the Ho Chi Minh trail in the Highlands of Vietnam.

ABOVE: A bomb explosion in a U.S. Army vehicle in Saigon on Christmas Eve 1964.

delivery-forward observers and some supplies, and also to evacuate the wounded, the primitive state of helicopter technology at this time preventing more ambitious roles. The USA was currently locked in the Cold War, the planners of the Department of Defense were focussed on the nuclear battlefield of the future, and at this juncture discovered that the U.S. Army needed a light reconnaissance aircraft organic to combat formations. The well-established Cessna L-19 (later O-1) Bird Dog was unsuitable for the task now considered and, to make matters worse, the still comparatively new U.S. Air Force feared the emergence of a new army air corps with large aircraft.

The USAF secured the support of large numbers of U.S. lawmakers concerned about the cost implications, stymying the U.S.

Army's ambitions in this regard. By the mid-1950s a pair of senior paratroopers, Lieutenant General James M. Gavin and Colonel (later Lieutenant General) John J. Tolson started to investigate the helicopter as the means of bypassing the USAF's concerns about the U.S. Army's use of large fixed-wing aircraft while still providing the U.S. Army with the reconnaissance capability it so clearly needed. Gavin and his staff thereupon proposed a new U.S. Cavalry, but in this instance carrying out its task on "lying horses." Gavin sent Tolson to Fort Benning as head of the Airborne School to work out a doctrine for the efficient use of helicopters and, in parallel, Brigadier General Carl I. Hutton and Colonel Jay D. Vanderpool were proceeding along the same line at the Army Aviation School at nearby Fort Rucker,

America's First Major Offensive

ABOVE: Members of the U.S. 1st Cavalry Division begin patrol duty from a helicopter landing base in 1965.

OPPOSITE: A UH-1D (Huey) Medevac helicopter takes off to pick up an injured member of the 101st Airborne Division, near the demilitarized zone.

The Helicopter in the Vietnam war

Alabama. Vanderpool managed to obtain the use of some helicopters, armed them with locally improved weapon systems, and by 1957 was testing his "Sky-Cavalry" platoon as a precursor to future divisions built round this radical concept.

The various aviation research projects by the Ordnance, Transportation and Signal Corps were coordinated at Fort Rucker to some extent, and in 1959 the U.S. Army gave the U.S. aviation industry guidelines to develop a "light observation, manned surveillance, and tactical transport aircraft." In fact the Bell company was already well advanced in the development of a turbine-powered utility helicopter, the Model 204, which later became the UH-1 Iroquois, or "Huey," helicopter workhorse of the Vietnam War. By this stage in the proceedings, many

U.S. Army officers looked on army aviation development in very positive terms, and the Rogers Board urged that each division be allocated helicopters with a tactical radius at least as great as the farthest reach of that divisional artillery. Nevertheless, the helicopter development program was very slow until a time early in

The U.S. Ground War in Vietnam 1965–1973

1962, when Secretary of Defense Robert McNamara pronounced the whole effort to date to have been "dangerously conservative." The U.S. Army aviators leapt at the challenge and, within 90 days of its establishment, the Howze Board, led by the U.S. Army's first director of aviation, presented McNamara with a 3,500-page report recommending five new divisions, each with an organic strength of 459 helicopters. The Huey would undertake the tactical deployment of troops, the new Boeing CH-47 Chinook twin-rotor medium-lift helicopter would carry the division's artillery of Honest John rockets and 105-mm (4.13-inch) howitzers, the intelligence branch would have some fixed-wing aircraft with cameras or radar, and a new, and currently nonexistent attack helicopter gunship would complete the requirements for the "air assault division" by suppressing enemy fire on and around the landing zone (LZ) for the Huey machines, before providing the landed troops with light fire support.

McNamara agreed with the concept, and the 11th Air Assault Division was formed at Fort Benning in January 1963. By a time late in 1964 it was common to see flights of Huey helicopters progressing at 115mph (185km/h) just a few feet above the trees. Five Huey gunships first broke over the planned LZ, raking it and the surrounding area with sustained rocket and machine gun fire. After another pass, the Huey gunships climbed to circle as seven other Huey helicopters, echeloned vertically, dropped into the LZ, disgorged their troops, and rapidly lifted off as the landed men raced to their rallying points off the LZ. As the first troopships rose in a swirl of dust, more arrived until an infantry company or more was on the ground, concentrated, and moving toward its objective. The commander overhead in his command and control machine had brought a substantial force from miles away to be "injected" deep into enemy territory with total surprise, and all in fewer than 15 minutes. This

The U.S. Ground War in Vietnam 1965–1973

air-mobility concept clearly worked, and would prove as necessary a development for the Vietnam War as airborne doctrine had been for the Second World War.

By the spring of 1965 Lieutenant General Charles Rich had finished his tests for the Howze Board, and had been so impressed by the efforts of the 11th Air Assault Division that he wished to keep it in existence as an operational formation. The Department of Defense concurred, and with the approval of General Creighton W. Abrahams, the Vice Chief of Staff, the 11th Air Assault Division was reconstituted as a cavalry formation – the 1st Cavalry Division (Airmobile).

In South Vietnam, meanwhile, the US was seeking to persuade the South Vietnamese military and civil administration, based on the urban elite, to take a greater interest in the "hearts and minds" of the rural population in a countryside increasingly dominated by the Viet Cong and its sympathizers. The USA also pushed forward the Cheu Hoi scheme to rehabilitate cooperative Viet Cong and North Vietnamese army prisoners and deserters, and sought to promote the creation of an urban bourgeoisie which would identify its new-found prosperity with the South Vietnamese government and therefore support it. It was an impossible task, for the corruption and nepotism of the

OPPOSITE: Members of the 4th Battalion, 503rd Regiment of the 101st Airborne Division board an American Airlines Astrojet at Fort Campbell, Kentucky, for the first leg of their flight to Vietnam in June 1966.

RIGHT: Christmas 1965: the comedian Bob Hope with Ann-Margret boosts morale onboard the USS *New Jersey*.

America's First Major Offensive

The U.S. Ground War in Vietnam 1965–1973

South Vietnamese administration, whoever was running it, was a national cancer that persuaded everyone to look after himself. For the South Vietnamese in general it was a case of seeking survival and advantage wherever this could be obtained, and to many this meant collaboration with both the South Vietnamese administration and the Communist insurgency. America put enormous effort and huge resources into its effort to reform and stabilize South Vietnamese society, but the Viet Cong was quietly rampant in rural areas. The South Vietnamese army undertook countless patrol operations, but the Viet Cong faded from sight whenever threatened, only to re-emerge as soon as the coast was clear. Thus the Viet Cong and North Vietnamese army continued to run their now well established shadow governments and effectively control the rural population.

The Communist political and military machine had the benefit of an excellent intelligence apparatus, which was so pervasive that most South Vietnamese operations were known, at least in part, before they began. Unless they were fortunate, most South Vietnamese patrols returned to their compounds empty-handed and with a number of dead and wounded from ambush, or perhaps a few "suspects," the latter generally seized arbitrarily from the rural population, whose sense of alienation from the government was thereby strengthened.

As part of the U.S. assistance scheme, General Taylor had as early as 1961 recommended there be greater use of U.S. air assets. Advisers soon saw, in

LEFT: Members of the 2nd Battalion, 3rd U.S. Marine Division vacating helicopters during an operation to penetrate Viet Cong territory outside the dense perimeter of Da Nang airbase in South Vietnam.

the resulting delivery of Vertol (Piasecki) H-21 Shawnee twin-rotor helicopters, the opportunity to gain a tactical advantage over the Viet Cong and so win back the element of surprise. U.S. training and equipment had improved both the skills and, to a lesser extent, the morale of the South Vietnamese army, and the U.S. advisers saw in the newly arrived helicopters the possibility of trapping Communist forces and preventing their escape, so forcing them to fight on terms advantageous to the matériel-richer South Vietnamese forces. On December 24, 1961 1,000 South Vietnamese troops were helicoptered into a suspected Viet Cong stronghold near Saigon, where they routed a small Viet Cong detachment.

The U.S. advisers saw this as heralding a new dawn, but there were only a few helicopters available and the great majority of South Vietnamese soldiers still moved on foot along the often-mined paddyfield dykes and roads between booby trapped tree lines. By 1965 the South Vietnamese army had still not been able to devise and implement any means of pinning down and destroying sizeable Communist forces, and the U.S. therefore decided to commit its airborne forces to tip the scale.

In May 1965 the 173rd Airborne Brigade from Okinawa landed in Vietnam. The brigade, commanded by Brigadier General Ellis W. Williamson, knew of the air-mobility

The U.S. Ground War in Vietnam 1965–1973

OPPOSITE: With the arrival of the 173rd Airborne Brigade from Okinawa on May 5, 1965, SP4 Archie L. Gaffee plots a fire mission for the 81-mm mortar squads.

ABOVE: As members of the 2nd Battalion, 503rd Infantry, 173rd Airborne Brigade launch a large-scale operation against the Viet Cong, 7.5 miles (12km) north of Bien Hoa airfield, artillery troops prepare to fire 81-mm mortars in support of advancing troops during an assault on an area heavily infested with Viet Cong.

developments at Fort Benning, and with the helicopters available to him started to train his men in the new air-mobility tactics At first, the paratroopers were unconvinced of these new tactical concepts, but confidence and coordination improved. When the 173rd Airborne Brigade was joined by the 1st Battalion Royal Australian Regiment and a battery of gunners from the Royal New Zealand Artillery, plus two more airborne battalions from Tolson's parent unit, the 503rd

Parachute Infantry Regiment, its men started to mount successful air-mobile operations. One of the first of these, near the Dong Nai river, resulted in the deaths of 56 Communist soldiers, the capture of 28 more men, and the seizure of hundreds of tons of rice and documents.

The North Vietnamese army was at the same time preparing its offensive to cut South Vietnam in two with an eastward offensive from the mountains to the sea. Commanding the Western Highlands Field Front,

49

America's First Major Offensive

transport vessels. Fortunately, elements of the 101st Airborne Division had also been alerted for deployment to South Vietnam, and arrived in time to secure the landing place for the 1st Cavalry Division (Airmobile). U.S. airborne units had already led the way into South Vietnam, and proved the worth of the new air-mobile tactics in cordon and search operations. Now the 1st Cavalry Division (Airmobile) was to head west from An Khe to test air-mobility in action against a large and militarily sophisticated force.

On October 19, 1965 the Communist forces kicked off the Tau Nguyen campaign by hitting the Plei Me Special Forces camp about 19 miles (30km) to the south of the provincial capital, Pleiku. Westmoreland ordered Major General H.W.O Kinnard to take his 1st Cavalry Division (Airmobile) to help in the South Vietnamese army's operation to relieve the camp and pursue the Communist attack force, but when the division's 1st Brigade arrived, the Communist forces had, as usual, melted away. Kinnard and his intelligence staff felt the Communists had probably fallen back to their base area and dispatched the division's Air Cavalry Squadron to locate them.

Operating at low level in an area of forests and ravines, the Hughes

LEFT: A humorous reminder to troops to take their medication.

OPPOSITE: Members of Company B, 2nd Battalion, 173rd Airborne Brigade apply blacking to their faces prior to beginning a search-and-destroy mission in the infamous Zone D, 12 miles (19km) south-east of Bien Hoa. The mission of the 173rd was to provide defense of the airfield and to assist ARVN forces when called upon to do so by the Vietnamese government.

General Chu Nuy Man planned a major thrust from Cambodia and the traditional Communist lurking grounds in west-central Vietnam along the Ia Drang river straight through four provinces to the sea. Intelligence suggested that this effort would start during the summer or fall of 1965, at a time when Rich had finished testing his air assault division. Thus the new 1st Cavalry Division (Airmobile) was available and was sent by sea to deploy its 16,000 men, 1,600 vehicles, and some 400 aircraft in the central part of South Vietnam.

The division's move in eight weeks presupposed an administrative landing, but its component units were then advised that they might have to fight their way ashore with their mothballed helicopters left on the decks of the

OH-6 light observation helicopters gained contact 6 miles (10km) west of the camp, which led to the capture of a North Vietnamese army field hospital. In the fighting for the hospital and in their sweeps, the relatively inexperienced U.S. soldiers learned that the units of the North Vietnamese army were well equipped – also skilled and determined. Wherever the U.S. forces established a perimeter, the North Vietnamese crawled so close that defending fire was rendered ineffective; they also sniped and otherwise harassed the U.S. soldiers at distances of 10 yards (9m) or less. The men of the 1st Cavalry Division learned swiftly, however, and in the hospital fight killed 78 North Vietnamese soldiers, taking 57 prisoners at the loss of five of their own men killed and 17 wounded.

By this stage of the Communist offensive, both South Vietnamese and U.S. intelligence were now sure that the Communist main body was moving west through the Ia Drang valley toward the Chu Pong mountains on the South Vietnamese side of the border, a region that had been a safe staging area for the North Vietnamese over a considerable time. On November 2, 1965 the 1st Squadron, 9th Cavalry Regiment flew into a small clearing, designated LZ "Mary," setting up an ambush on the side of the hills running down from the Chu Pong massif toward the Ia Drang river. This was the division's first attempt at a night air-mobile ambush, and was supported by a company of infantry also brought at night. The ambush led to the Communist loss of 150 North Vietnamese killed, and to U.S. losses of four killed, and 25 wounded. The inescapable conclusion was that the Communist main body was located in this area, and having

America's First Major Offensive

HO CHI MINH TRAIL

One of the most difficult problems facing the U.S. and South Vietnamese forces was the network of extemporized roads, tracks, and paths collectively known as the Ho Chi Minh Trail. Passing from North Vietnam into neutral Laos and Cambodia, it offered the Communists a veritable mass of avenues along which to pass men, matériel, and supplies. The trail was virtually undetectable, except in miniscule portions, impossible to sever, being possessed of so many tentacles, and lay largely in neutral countries.

The name for the trail was taken from North Vietnam's leader Ho Chi Minh. The trail was built and excavated by hand. Intricate tunnels with concealed entrances hid trekkers often directly under the feet of American troops searching for them. The trail undeniably lay at the heart of the war. For the Vietnamese of the North, the trail symbolized the aspirations of its people. Despite millions of bombs being dropped the trail remained consistently in operation.

laid the groundwork, the air cavalry turned over the completion of the task to the infantry.

By November 9 Chu Nuy Man's forces were located in two major staging areas, with the 32nd North Vietnamese Regiment on the northern bank of the Ia Drang and quite close to the South Vietnamese/Cambodian frontier, with the high-quality 66th North Vietnamese Regiment and the less capable 33rd between the river and the eastern slope of the Chu Pong massif. The 33rd North Vietnamese Regiment had lost about one third of its original strength of 2,200 men in the fighting for Plei Me, and was now revised as a composite battalion, albeit still of nearly regimental size. The division's 120-mm (4.72 inch) mortars and 14.5-mm (0.57 inch) twin-barrel antiaircraft machine guns were still on the Ho Chi Minh Trail in Cambodia, but Chu was happy with his formation's security on the rocky and wooded slopes of the area and prepared another attack on Plei Me.

The search for the North Vietnamese position was entrusted to Colonel T.W. Brown's 3rd Brigade and the 1st Cavalry Division. The 3rd Brigade included, among its maneuver battalions, two from the famous 7th US Cavalry. Much of the brigade had trained together in the 11th Air Assault Division experiments and had excellent morale. The brigade began to search the valley by setting-down squads and platoons in a process of so-called saturation patrolling, but the search area near the massif appeared so promising that Lieutenant Colonel H.G. Moore, commanding the 1st Battalion, 7th Cavalry, decided to look for an LZ where he could set-down the whole of his battalion. On the morning of November 14 Moore reconnoitred the area from the air in an apparently casual manner, and in the process evaluated three possible LZs before opting for the largest of these, which had the size to accommodate eight to ten helicopters simultaneously. From the air the LZ appeared to be moderately open, with tall, brown, elephant grass beneath scrub trees of up to 100 feet (30m) high, even though the terrain undulated and was dotted with anthills about 8 feet (2.4m) high. The woods grew denser toward Chu Pong, and a dry stream-bed extended along the western edge of what would become LZ "X-Ray."

On returning to his base camp, Moore dispatched an OH-6 helicopter to check the area once again. When the helicopter's crew reported seeing communications wire in the area of LZ X-Ray, Moore ordered his battalion to mount up. At 10:17am two 105-mm

The U.S. Ground War in Vietnam 1965–1973

LEFT: Booby traps were a common danger in the Vietnam War. It was a device setup to kill, maim, or surprise a victim, who was often lured towards it.

BELOW: Troops of the 173rd Airborne Brigade, with full field equipment and two army mules, march from the airfield to their defensive area on their arrival in Zone D.

(4.13 inch) howitzer batteries of the 1st Battalion, 21st Artillery, located some 5.5 miles (8.8 km) east of LZ X-Ray, began a 20-minute barrage of preparatory fire onto LZ X-Ray and, for purposes of deception, the two other possible LZs. The aerial rocket artillery of the 2nd Battalion, 20th Artillery, lifted off and the second the last artillery projectile detonated, the helicopters swept in and over a period

America's First Major Offensive

of some 30 seconds expended half their loads on LZ X-Ray before climbing and waiting near the LZ ready for any call for more support. The escorting gunships of "A" Company, 229th Aviation Battalion, raked the area before "B" Company landed with Moore in personal command. By 10:48am the helicopters were returning to collect and deliver A Company, and at much the same time Moore's operations officer, artillery liaison officer, and USAF forward air controller arrived overhead to call in artillery and tactical air attacks as necessary, and to relay radio communications if required.

Once he was on the ground, the commander of "B" Company detached small parties off to check the tree line, while holding the bulk of his company in a thicket on the LZ to react to any sign of Communist activity. At 11:20am, a North Vietnamese army deserter was brought in and told Moore that the U.S. company was faced by at least three fully-prepared North Vietnamese army battalions. Chu had, in fact, already started his movement toward Plei Me when the landings were reported, and immediately positioned his 33rd and 66th North Vietnamese Regiments to the west of Chu Pong and along its base in a totally silent, very rapid movement in less than one hour. B Company continued searching to the north-east

ABOVE: Cam Canh Bay port, Vietnam.

OPPOSITE: Lt. Gen William C. Westmoreland tours the fishing village of Vam Lang during his first orientation trip to the area. He became the new commander of the Military Advisory Command, Vietnam (MACV), on August 1, 1964.

of the LZ along a spur extending from the mountain, with two platoons abreast and the third platoon in reserve behind the left-hand platoon. As the left-hand platoon came off the spur and crossed a dry stream-bed, it moved slightly ahead of the right-hand platoon and was suddenly taken under heavy and accurate small arms fire from an estimated North Vietnamese platoon hidden in the grass. Both flanks of the U.S. platoons were exposed, and the commander of B Company responded by ordering the reserve to press forward, sending the right-hand platoon over to the right flank of the pinned platoon.

As soon as the right-hand platoon received the order, a skirmish line was formed with a 7.62-mm (0.3 inch) M60 machine gun on each flank, and started to work its way toward the firing. As the platoon advanced, its reserve squad, in the rear, saw about 20 North Vietnamese soldiers disappear behind anthills on its left flank, between the place where it was and the location at which it hoped to find the left-hand platoon. The reserve squad's grenadier immediately fired a series of 40-mm grenades from his M79 launcher into the anthills, but was then cut down by a burst of fire from his right. This signaled a major firefight and the right-hand platoon now found itself in difficulty. The platoon leader dispatched his two machine gun crews to cover the reserve squad, the rest of the platoon forming a tight perimeter which was taken under North Vietnamese mortar and rocket fire. Soon the reserve squad and one of the machine gun crews ran into the comparative safety of the perimeter carrying the dead grenadier's launcher. The other four-man machine gun team did not make it and the North Vietnamese soon brought the captured gun to bear on the platoon.

As the weight of fire increased, the commander of B Company attempted to report the situation to Moore, with emphasis on the situation to his front, but the trees, tall grass, and smoke severely curtailed his ability to discern what was happening. As he reported, Moore and his radio operator themselves came under fire, and one North Vietnamese soldier got to within 15 yards (14m) before the commander of B Company stopped him with grenade and rifle fire. The company commander was now sure that his left-hand platoon, which had been the original object for rescue, had now to become the rescuer after the reserve platoon had joined it.

Meanwhile, Moore set up his command post at the LZ and was bringing in A Company to the left to protect B Company's flank, imagining that the two left-hand platoons of B Company would be exposed as they turned to assist the isolated platoon. It was now about 1:30pm and the first men of "C" Company were landing. Moore sent them to cover A Company by taking positions just off the LZ to the south and south-west. The rear of Moore's position was not covered, and mortar fire was falling on the LZ, but he could do little else. Meanwhile, the rest of C Company and the whole of "D" Company had not yet landed.

Second Lieutenant Walter J. Marm of A Company landed and quickly moved his platoon off the LZ in a skirmish line toward the sound of

ABOVE: Soldiers of the U.S. Army 1/7th Cavalry disembark from a Bell UH-1D Huey at LZ X-Ray during the battle of Ia Drang.

OPPOSITE: Combat operations at Ia Drang Valley, Vietnam, November 1965. Major Bruce P. Crandall's UH-1D helicopter climbs skyward after discharging a load of infantrymen on a search and destroy mission.

firing. He almost immediately took two prisoners, and soon linked up with B Company's reserve platoon. With it Marm planned to make for the trapped platoon, but then his command and the reserve platoon came under heavy fire. The same North Vietnamese unit which had tried to cut off the right-hand B Company was now apparently moving to surround the whole of B Company and also Marm's A Company platoon. As they returned fire, Marm tried to evacuate his wounded, but the sergeant detailed for the mission reported that he could not get through. The North Vietnamese force then broke off and moved down into the dry stream-bed in an effort to circle behind Marm, but in so doing ran into the rest of A Company as it came up from the LZ. Fierce combat broke out in the stream-bed and on its banks, and a platoon leader and squad leader of "AS" Company were among the first men to be killed.

As A and B Companies lay in several exposed positions, Moore and the circling artillery and USAF officers tried to assist. The company's mortars had long since expended their basic load and the area was shrouded in dust and smoke. The pinned cavalrymen had no prominent landmarks they could use to indicate the positions of themselves and the North Vietnamese, and therefore could not call in effective fire in their own support. The heliborne officers could do little but guess at the friendly positions, and brought down artillery fire and air attacks as close as they dared. The 33rd and 66th North Vietnamese Regiments were in firm control of the situation, and the fire became so heavy that they managed to shoot down a Douglas A-1 Skyraider attack warplane, whose pilot was killed. Despite the fact that the LZ was "hot," most especially in its north-western sector nearest the spur, the 1st Battalion's surgeon was able to arrive by air at 2:00pm. The doctor made it to the command post and with four medical aidmen began to treat the mounting number of wounded who had made it back to the command post.

Knowing the risks, the division's helicopters nonetheless arrived on a fifth airlift with the rest of C Company and the first part of "D" Company. As the helicopters landed and their troops disembarked, the most severely wounded were rushed into the first helicopters, but a pilot and door gunner were wounded before they could lift off. The commander of D Company was creased by a bullet, and his radio operator was killed before he could unfasten his seatbelt. In the face of such fire, Moore ordered that the rest of D Company should not land. The commander of D Company now managed to get the radio from the operator's body and ran off the LZ with four men, who soon found themselves to the right of A Company's two platoons, which were now fighting the North Vietnamese, discovered by Marm as they were attempting to encircle B Company to his front. The commander of D Company summoned the rest of his men from the LZ and, as they came into position, warned them that there were North Vietnamese soldiers already to the rear, where the commander and his men had just been. Then, without any warning, the small command group found itself the focus of North Vietnamese fire: several men were killed, and the commander of D Company and his mortar platoon

ABOVE: The Duc My Ranger Training Center in Vietnam. Captain Samuel W. Smith, infantry adviser, Tactics Committee Advisory Team, RTC, Major Bill T. Thompson, senior adviser, RTC; and 2nd Lt. Pham Xuan Triem, chief, PT section, watch 2nd Lt. Nguyen Quany Canh indicate ways of reacting to different combat situations.

OPPOSITE: The same team leading a patrol of Vietnamese rangers-in-training on the Platoon Reaction Course.

leader were severely wounded. By now it was 3:00pm, and Moore placed C Company, completed by the arrival of the fifth airlift, as a blocking force along the right flank of A Company. The men rushed into position and were soon under intense North Vietnamese fire.

The brigade commander now arrived overhead and Moore told him that he was being attacked by about 600 North Vietnamese troops, with every possibility of reinforcement. Moore called for another rifle company, a request which Brown had anticipated, and B Company, 2nd Battalion, 7th Cavalry was ready for insertion as soon as the LZ cooled down. Two helicopters in the last flight had been so damaged that they could not fly, and lay off to the side of the LZ, their crews having been collected by other helicopters. Brown's main contribution, at this time, was to land his 2nd Battalion, 5th Cavalry at LZ "Victor," some 1.9 miles (3km) to the south-east of LZ X-Ray. Here the battalion was to dig in for the night before moving out toward Moore's force during the following morning.

In the middle of the afternoon Moore noticed that the employment of C and D Companies was reducing the amount of North Vietnamese fire sweeping the LZ, and as fast as he could personally guided in the last three loads of C Company, the Scout (reconnaissance) platoon, a Pathfinder team, and the executive officer and first D Company. Up on the line A and B Companies had pulled back to coordinate, while C and D Companies

America's First Major Offensive

held the perimeter with the aid of artillery fire on trajectories at right angles to the air attacks. The North Vietnamese lay only yards away from the isolated platoon, so close that the men could not raise their arms to dig for cover. The platoon leader and platoon sergeant were among the eight men who had been killed. The next senior, Sergeant Savage, and his medic displayed great leadership in rallying the seven unwounded and 12 wounded, many of the latter remaining on the line.

Because the 7th Cavalry was airmobile, and could therefore carry more per man, it was policy for every man to carry more than 300 rounds for his 5.56-mm (0.22 inch) M16 rifle, at least two fragmentation grenades, two canteens of water, and one ration packet. Each grenadier carried about 30 grenades and each machine gunner had at least 800 rounds for his M60. Most men carried more than this, so unless they were overrun by superior numbers, the isolated platoon stood every chance of holding on.

ABOVE: Candidates practice jumping out of a C-47 mock-up during a training course at the Vietnamese Army Jump School, Airborne Brigade Headquarters, Camp Hoang Hoa Tham, near Tan Son Nhut airbase, Saigon. The school was fashioned after the U.S. Army Jump School at Fort Benning, Georgia, and was commanded by Captain Tran Van Vinh.

Moore issued a preparatory order to A and B Companies to attack and bring in the platoon. At 4:20pm the two companies moved forward from the stream-bed after artillery and air artillery preparation had been brought in as close as 275 yards (250m) to B Company's front. It made little difference. The North Vietnamese had quietly moved up almost to the tops of the stream-bank. Hiding in anthills and trees, they were fully ready when the two companies moved out. The ensuing fight was terrible for the Americans: Marm's platoon was stopped by a machine gun just 30 yards (27m) to its front but concealed in the grass. Marm raised himself out of cover in an effort to pinpoint its location, and when his sergeant's grenade fell short, Marm raced out, scooped it up, and hurled it into the machine gun nest, dispatching the remaining crew with his rifle. However, the loss of the machine gun did little to change the overall situation in favor of the Americans. U.S. casualties continued to mount, and as most of A Company's leaders had been killed or wounded, Moore told the company it had his permission to fall back to the LZ. It had moved only 165 yards (150m).

B Company was also receiving fire, so heavy that it had taken 30 casualties and had to pull back. But the North Vietnamese fire was such that neither company could retreat. A Company's forward observer had been killed and no smoke rounds were available to cover the withdrawal, but Moore recalled how effective white phosphorus rounds had been in the Korean War. Soon the 1st Battalion, 21st Artillery launched a barrage of WP shells, and the star-like bursts of burning phosphorus over the North Vietnamese positions provided the two battered companies with just sufficient time to crawl back with their casualties.

Between 5:00pm and 7:00pm Moore created as tight a perimeter as he could. Defensive artillery and mortar patterns were coordinated and Moore chose part of the LZ, enough for two helicopters, as his last stand. The 229th Pathfinders (men skilled at guiding in aircraft or paratroops onto improvised landing sites) cleared this final LZ of trees with engineer demolition charges and marked out the lighting panels for nightfall; they were under fire the whole time without suffering any casualties. Around them the exhausted and thirsty cavalrymen dug prone positions and ate the jam from their rations for its moisture. They were heartened when B Company of the 2nd Battalion suddenly swooped in, as promised by Brown, and at 7:15pm a re-supply mission skidded in with its crews, pushing out ammunition, water, rations, and literally vital medical supplies. Soon after this, the operations officer landed with his two fire controllers, but that was the last movement of the day. The remains of the 1st Battalion, 7th Cavalry lay under a thick pall of smoke and darkness, awaiting the North Vietnamese troops' next move.

The isolated platoon could not move: Savage adjusted artillery to within yards of his position by radio, and soon the 1st Battalion, 21st Artillery knew exactly where Savage's perimeter was. The North Vietnamese attacked three times before 3:45am, the sound of their bugle calls coming from the mountain 330 yards (300m) away, indicating the imminence of another attack. As Savage heard the North Vietnamese speaking, he called down a 15-minute barrage with air strikes under illumination. The North Vietnamese retreated slightly, but the light played over the Americans and they had to drive back another major assault in darkness about one hour later.

The main perimeter had also been probed. The 66th North Vietnamese Regiment's 8th Battalion had by now arrived. At first light on November 15 Moore called his commanders together to plan the relief of Savage's platoon. Moore also ordered a thorough check to a distance of 220 yards (200m) made outside the perimeter. Although the Americans did not know it, during the night the North Vietnamese had crawled through the exploding artillery right up to the U.S. perimeter. As the first troopers moved out to sweep around the perimeter, they ran into a withering crossfire. Some men rushed out to help those who had fallen and were themselves hit, and within the space of seconds the commander of C Company and two of his lieutenants had been severely wounded by a machine gun not 45 yards (40m) to their front. Moore now ordered a platoon of A Company to cross the LZ in support of C Company. The commander of A Company took the platoon farthest away from contact, closed the gap with his other men, and dispatched the platoon, which lost two men killed and two wounded as it tried to cross the LZ. The other men of the platoon dropped to a prone position on line between the right flank of C Company and the left flank of their own unit. From there they provided defense in depth and protected the command post and aid station in the event that the perimeter was overrun.

The firing on the perimeter defense became dense as D Company, on the left flank of C Company, was attacked. At 7:45am rockets, mortars, and automatic weapons fire sealed the LZ. The 7th Cavalry replied to all these new thrusts with all the firepower it had, and large numbers of North Vietnamese were killed. The fighting had grown so desperate by 7:55am that Moore had each platoon mark its position with colored smoke, for though this advertised the position to the North Vietnamese, it also marked it for the pilots of the attack aircraft to drop bombs and napalm. These were aimed so close that some accidentally dropped inside the perimeter, ignited the reserve ammunition, and burned two men. By this time, the North Vietnamese had pinpointed the position of the consolidated mortars, and now put some of them out of action. Moore had no choice but to ask Brown again for another company. At 9:10am A Company, 2nd Battalion was delivered in heavy fire, and the fresh troopers went into line alongside their own B Company.

Finally, at 10:00am, the tons of ordnance from the air attacks and artillery barrages began to achieve results, and the North Vietnamese reduced the pressure of their onslaught to mere harassing fire. This gave the cavalrymen a breathing space to distribute ammunition, move the newly-wounded back to the command post, and then to wait once more. Fortunately, the 2nd Battalion, 5th Cavalry was now completing its approach march from LZ "Victor" and, after only light resistance, was able to enter LZ X-Ray at about 12:00pm, bringing the total U.S. strength to about nine companies, four of which had been hard hit.

Moore coordinated with the arriving battalion commander, Lieutenant Colonel R.B. Tully. The first task was the recovery of the isolated platoon and, as it knew the way, B Company of the 2nd Battalion, 7th Cavalry was detailed to lead Tully toward Savage at 13:15pm, while Tully's A and C Companies provided the muscle. In an attempt to divert attention from Tully, Moore mounted another sweep all around the perimeter and scoured the interior, too, in case any North Vietnamese had managed to infiltrate. The troops moved through the blood-stained grass to find North Vietnamese dead stacked up behind anthills. There were craters of churned earth, fragments of North Vietnamese uniforms, and the trails leading toward Chu Pong were soaked in blood and littered with equipment. The unsuccessful sweep of the morning left its evidence of dead American soldiers surrounded by dead North Vietnamese.

LEFT: His hands tied at his waist, a wounded Viet Cong prisoner is forced by his captors, South Vietnamese government forces, to wade through a stream near Bac Lieu in the Mekong delta area as a human detector against mines and booby traps. The guerrilla, recently captured in Operation Eagle Flight by a government ranger battalion, later died from his wounds.

OPPOSITE: A Viet Cong suspect, captured during an attack on an American outpost near the Cambodian border in South Vietnam, is interrogated.

The U.S. Ground War in Vietnam 1965–1973

America's First Major Offensive

Tully advanced without incident up the spur and located the much-relieved lost platoon. In slow order and with only one serious casualty from a sniper, the complete party now retired in good order down to the LZ, carrying the dead and wounded. Once it reached the perimeter, the 2nd Battalion, 5th Cavalry moved to assume an equal share of the defense and everyone dug in.

The cavalrymen had not been forgotten by higher command echelons, and during the afternoon a B-52 raid was made against Chu Pong itself: this was also of significance being the first occasion on which the strategic bombers had been used for the tactical support of ground forces. Throughout the following night, even though artillery ringed the perimeter in depth, the North Vietnamese nonetheless managed to probe the line, finally launching a company-sized attack against B Company of the 2nd Battalion at 05:30 and again an hour later.

To avoid falling into the same trap as the day before, Moore instructed the entire perimeter to fire all its weapons into the trees, anthills, and elephant grass at first light, in a "mad minute" of firing. This proved a successful ploy: snipers fell from the trees only a few yards from the cavalry, and a platoon-sized attack was prematurely triggered. After a pause, Moore decided to sweep out to 550 yards (500m), and while doing so B Company of the 2nd Battalion again took the brunt of a determined attack by wounded North Vietnamese, who hurled grenades from where they had fallen. Firing all the way, the company fell back into the perimeter and the forward air controller called in air attacks so close that a 500 pound (227-kg) bomb was delivered on target only 25 yards (23m) in front of the perimeter.

The North Vietnamese were now exhausted, and another U.S. sweep met with little opposition. The LZ was now safe enough for the rest of the 2nd Battalion's companies to land and Moore's weary troopers were carried out. Moore's command had accounted for 634 North Vietnamese known dead and another 581 estimated killed, and six prisoners had been taken. Despite their aversion to abandoning any weapons, the North Vietnamese left more than 100 crew-served and individual weapons, including four Maxim machine guns, rocket launchers, and mortars. Moore's losses were 79 killed and 121 wounded.

ABOVE: A USAF North American F-100D-20-NA Super Sabre of the 481st Tactical Fighter Squadron pulls up sharply after releasing a napalm bomb on Viet Cong concealed in the tree line in the Mekong Delta. The 481st TFS was deployed to Tan Son Nhut Airbase, Vietnam, from June to November 1965.

OPPOSITE: U.S. An Khe Army Airfield under construction in 1965.

The battle seemed to be over, and there appeared to be no reason for the US forces to remain in the field. The mission was complete and arguably a success, but Brown was concerned about reports that additional North Vietnamese units were moving into the area over the border. Brown wished to withdraw his command but Westmoreland demanded that the 2nd Battalion, 7th Cavalry and 1st Battalion, 5th Cavalry remain at LZ X-Ray, so that there would be no appearance of retreat.

On the following day the two remaining battalions abandoned LZ X-Ray and began moving to new landing zones: the 2nd/5th under Tully "Columbus" about 2.5 miles (4km) to the north-east, and the 2nd/7th under Lieutenant Colonel Robert McDade to LZ "Albany," about the same distance to the north-north-east, close to the Ia Drang. B-52 bombers had already been dispatched from their base on Guam, their target being the slopes of the Chu Pong massif. The U.S. ground forces had to move outside a 2-mile (3.2-km) safety zone by mid-morning to be clear of the scheduled bombardment, and Tully's battalion moved out at 9:00am with McDade's Battalion following 10 minutes later.

The first sign of a Communist presence was detected by the U.S. column's point units, the point squad of the reconnaissance platoon under Staff Sergeant Donald J. Slovak, who saw "Ho Chi Minh sandal foot markings, bamboo arrows on the ground pointing north, matted grass, and grains of rice." After marching for about 2,200 yards (2000m), A Company leading the 2nd/7th headed north-west, while the 2nd/5th continued toward LZ Columbus. A Company came upon some grass huts which they were ordered to burn. At 11:38am the 2nd/5th reached LZ Columbus.

The Communist troops in the area consisted of the 8th Battalion of the 66th North Vietnamese Regiment, the 1st Battalion of the 33rd North Vietnamese Regiment, and the headquarters of the 3rd Battalion of the 33rd North Vietnamese Regiment. The 33rd North Vietnamese Regiment was below strength as a result of the casualties it had suffered during the battle at the Plei Me Special Forces camp, while the 8th Battalion was General An's reserve, and as such was fresh and rested.

A Company soon noticed the sudden absence of air cover and its commander, Captain Joel Sugdinis, wondered where the helicopters were.

He soon heard the sound of explosions to his rear, and knew that the B-52 bombers were unloading their bomb loads on the Chu Pong massif.

Leading the reconnaissance platoon, Lieutenant D.P. Payne was moving around some anthills when he came upon a North Vietnamese soldier resting on the ground and took him prisoner, while simultaneously, about 10 yards (9m) away, his platoon sergeant captured a second. Other members of the North Vietnamese reconnaissance team may have escaped and reported to the headquarters of the 1st Battalion, 33rd North Vietnamese Regiment, and it was at about this time that the

North Vietnamese began to plan and implement an attack on the U.S. column. As word of the two captured North Vietnamese reached him, McDade ordered a halt and moved up the column to undertake a personal interrogation. The captured soldiers were being held about 100 yards (90m) from the south-western edge of the clearing called Albany, the report of which reached division forward at Pleiku at 11:57am. McDade then called his company commanders together, most of them with their radio operators, for a conference. A Company moved forward to LZ Albany, McDade and his command group with it, and the other company commanders were moving forward to join McDade. D Company, which was following A Company, halted, and so did the following C Company which was next in line. The Battalion HQ Company followed, and A Company of the 1st Battalion, 5th Cavalry brought up the rear of the column. The U.S. column was thus extended in 550-yard (500-m) line. Most of the units had flank security posted, but the men were worn out from almost 60 hours without sleep and four hours of marching. The elephant grass was chest-high and visibility was limited.

Some 70 minutes after the two North Vietnamese soldiers had been captured, A Company and McDade's command group reached LZ Albany. McDade and his group walked across the clearing and into a clump of trees, beyond which was another clearing, while the remainder of the battalion was in a dispersed column to the east of the LZ. Battalion Sergeant Major James Scott and Sergeant Charles Bass then attempted to question the prisoners again. While they were doing this, Bass heard voices, and the interpreter confirmed they were hearing North Vietnamese troops talking. A Company had been in the LZ for about five minutes by this time, and at this moment small arms fire began. Payne's reconnaissance platoon .had walked to within 200 yards (180m) of the headquarters of the 3rd

ABOVE: Marines from the 1st Battalion, 3d Marines disembark from U.S. Air Force C-130 transports at the Da Nang Airbase on March 8, 1965. The airlift of the battalion was held up for 24 hours shortly after these Marines arrived.

OPPOSITE: Men of H Company, 2nd Battalion, 7th Marines, move along rice paddy dikes in pursuit of the Viet Cong.

Battalion, 33rd North Vietnamese Regiment. The 550 men of the 8th Battalion, 66th North Vietnamese Regiment had been resting off to the north-east of the U.S. column, and as the U.S. troopers rested in the tall grass, North Vietnamese soldiers were approaching them in some numbers. It was 1:15pm, and the engagement which followed lasted some 16 hours.

The North Vietnamese forces first struck at the head of the 2nd Battalion's column, spreading along the right or east side. The North Vietnamese soldiers ran down the length of the column, with units peeling off to attack the U.S. units. McDade's command group made it into the clump of trees between the two clearings of LZ Albany, and here took cover among the trees and anthills. The reconnaissance platoon and the 1st Platoon of A Company provided initial defense at this position, but by 1:26pm had been cut off from the rest of the column as North Vietnamese troops closed in around them. While they waited for air support, the U.S. troopers holding LZ Albany drove off assaults by the North Vietnamese, sniping at anyone they saw around the perimeter. Later, it was discovered that North Vietnamese soldiers had been mopping up, looking for U.S. wounded in the tall grass and killing them.

All the while the noise of battle could be heard in the woods as the other companies fought for their lives. C and A Companies lost 70 men between them in the first minutes, while C Company suffered 45 dead and more than 50 wounded, the heaviest casualties of any unit involved in the LZ Albany engagement. A-1E Skyraiders of the USAF were soon overhead to provide aerial fire support by dropping napalm. However, because of the smoke, dust, and the intermingling of the U.S. and North Vietnamese troops, it is likely that the air and artillery strikes killed Americans as well as North Vietnamese.

The 2nd Battalion, 7th Cavalry had been reduced to a small perimeter at LZ Albany, this containing the survivors of A Company, the reconnaissance platoon, the remnants of C and D

Companies, and the command group. There was also a smaller perimeter at the rear of the column about 500–700 yards (460–640m) due south around Captain George Forrest's A Company of the 1st Battalion, 5th Cavalry. Forrest had run a gauntlet all the way back from the conference called by McDade, when the North Vietnamese mortar fire began to plunge down on the Americans.

At 2.55pm, B Company of the 1st Battalion, 5th Cavalry under Captain Buse Tully began marching from LZ Columbus toward the rear of the 2nd Battalion, 7th Cavalry's column, about 2 miles (3.2km) distant. By 4:30pm, they had reached the A Company perimeter, where an LZ large enough for a single helicopter was secured and the wounded were evacuated. Tully's men then began to advance toward the rest of the ambushed column, all the while under North Vietnamese attack. After receiving fire from the tree line, Tully's men assaulted this and pushed back the North Vietnamese. At 6:25pm orders were received to secure into a two-company perimeter for the night, with the advance to resume from this coming in the morning.

At 4:00pm or thereabouts, Captain Myron Diduryk's B Company of the 2nd Battalion, 7th Cavalry, which had been at LZ X-Ray, was detailed for deployment in

ABOVE: Known Viet Cong prisoners are being led to a helicopter landing zone for evacuation to the regimental collection point. The men all have old bullet wounds and barbed-wire fence wounds.

the effort to relieve the trapped battalion. At 6:45pm the first troop-transport helicopters reached LZ Albany and the troopers were deployed into the tall grass. Lieutenant Rick Rescorla, the sole remaining platoon leader of B Company, led the reinforcements into Albany's perimeter, which was then enlarged to provide better security. LZ Albany's wounded were evacuated

The U.S. Ground War in Vietnam 1965–1973

at around 10:30pm that night, the helicopters involved coming under intense ground fire as they landed and took off. The U.S. troopers holding Albany then settled down for the night.

On the following day, November 18, the U.S. troopers started to collect their dead, a task which in fact lasted into the next day, the whole of the area being littered with dead Americans and North Vietnamese. On November 19, the U.S. troopers quit LZ Albany for LZ "Crooks," 6 miles (9.7km) away.

The engagement at LZ Albany cost the Americans 155 men killed and 124 wounded, bringing the overall toll for X-Ray and Albany fighting to 234 dead and 242 wounded. Within this fighting, the ambush of November 17 had been the costliest for the U.S. forces in the whole of the Vietnam War, with 155 killed and 126 wounded.

The battle can be regarded as a microcosm of the Vietnam War as a whole. The combination of air mobility for the troops with superior air and artillery firepower proved effective in allowing the U.S. forces to accomplish their tactical task. The North Vietnamese and Viet Cong forces learned, however, that they could offset the capabilities of U.S. firepower by closing right up to the American forces. The North Vietnamese later refined this tactic, which they called "grabbing the enemy by his belt" and with it achieved a kill/loss rate the Americans found politically unsustainable over anything but the very short term. For the time being, however, the North Vietnamese effort to cut South Vietnam in half had been prevented.

While it was a U.S. victory in arithmetical terms, as a result of the 4/1 casualty ratio in favor of the U.S. forces, many considered the battle to have been no more than a draw, since the U.S. Army left the field, allowing the North Vietnamese to reassert control over the area.

The lessons of the Ia Drang operation were clear: moderately inexperienced but well-trained troops could and did acquit themselves well in the face of hardened opponents. They were much aided by supporting fire and reinforcements, but the key factor was the helicopter, which could turn a surrounded force, isolated deep within enemy territory, into an active one with an effective supply line for resupply, reinforcement and evacuation of the wounded. The first engagement between U.S. troops and regular units of the North Vietnamese army, the Ia Drang operation also proved that the helicopter was not a fragile toy but a sturdy weapon.

The North Vietnamese division retreated across the border into Cambodia where, because of restrictions imposed by Washington, U.S. troops were forbidden to follow, and was soon reconstituted as a viable fighting force. The problem of the Communist forces taking refuge in Cambodia and Laos, rebuilding, then returning to fight again, was to trouble Westmoreland for a long time. Although Washington had approved ground patrols to locate the enemy just inside Laos and call in tactical air attacks, Westmoreland had no authority to pursue the Communist forces into Laos or to make any move against Communist sanctuaries in Cambodia. The Department of State refused every request from the MACV to patrol, bomb, or shell North Vietnamese extra-territorial camps. Although it was obvious that the Cambodian head of state, Prince Norodom Sihanouk, had tacitly sanctioned the Viet Cong and North Vietnamese presence in his country, the Department of State thought it better to tolerate that policy rather than risk driving Sihanouk into open collaboration with the Communists.

Text-Dependent Questions

1. What was Operation Starlite?

2. What model of helicopter became the workhorse of the Vietnam War?

3. How many American lives were lost at LZ Albany?

Research Projects

Why was the ground war in Vietnam so difficult for the Americans to fight?

TIME LINE OF THE VIETNAM WAR

1858 French colonial rule begins.

1930 Ho Chi Minh founds the Indochinese Communist Party (ICP).

1941 ICP organises a guerrilla force, Viet Minh, in response to invasion by Japan during World War II.

1945 The Viet Minh seizes power. Ho Chi Minh announces Vietnam's independence.

1946 French forces attack Viet Minh in Haiphong in November, sparking the war of resistance against the colonial power.

1950 Democratic Republic of Vietnam is recognised by China and USSR.

1954 Viet Minh forces attack an isolated French military outpost in the town of Dien Bien Phu. The attempt to take the outpost lasts two months, during which time the French government agrees to peace talks in Geneva.

Vietnam is split into North and South at Geneva conference.

1956 South Vietnamese President Ngo Dinh Diem begins campaign against political dissidents.

1957 Beginning of Communist insurgency in the South.

1959 Weapons and men from North Vietnam begin infiltrating the South.

1960 American aid to Diem increased.

1962 Number of U.S. military advisors in South Vietnam rises to 12,000.

1963 Viet Cong, the communist guerrillas operating in South Vietnam, defeat units of the ARVN, the South Vietnamese Army.

President Diem is overthrown and then killed in a U.S.-backed military coup.

U.S. ENTERS THE WAR

1964 Gulf of Tonkin incident: the U.S. says North Vietnamese patrol boats fire on two U.S. Navy destroyers. U.S. Congress approves Gulf of Tonkin Resolution, authorising military action in region.

1965 200,000 American combat troops arrive in South Vietnam.

1966 U.S. troop numbers in Vietnam rise to 400,000, then to 500,000 the following year.

1968 Tet Offensive - a combined assault by Viet Cong and the North Vietnamese army on U.S. positions - begins. More than 500 civilians die in the U.S. massacre at My Lai. Thousands are killed by communist forces during their occupation of the city of Hue.

1969 Ho Chi Minh dies. President Nixon begins to reduce U.S. ground troops in Vietnam as domestic public opposition to the war grows.

1970 Nixon's national security advisor, Henry Kissinger, and Le Duc Tho, for the Hanoi government, start talks in Paris.

1973 Cease-fire agreement in Paris, U.S. troop pull-out completed by March.

1975 North Vietnamese troops invade South Vietnam and take control of the whole country after South Vietnamese President Duong Van Minh surrenders.

OPPOSITE: A USAF Douglas A-1J Skyraider (U.S. Navy BuNo 142016) of the 6th Special Operations Squadron bombing a ground target in Vietnam. The 6th SOS operated from Pleiku and Da Nang air bases in 1968 and 1969. It was deactivated on November 15, 1969 and its aircraft were turned over to the South Vietnamese Air Force.

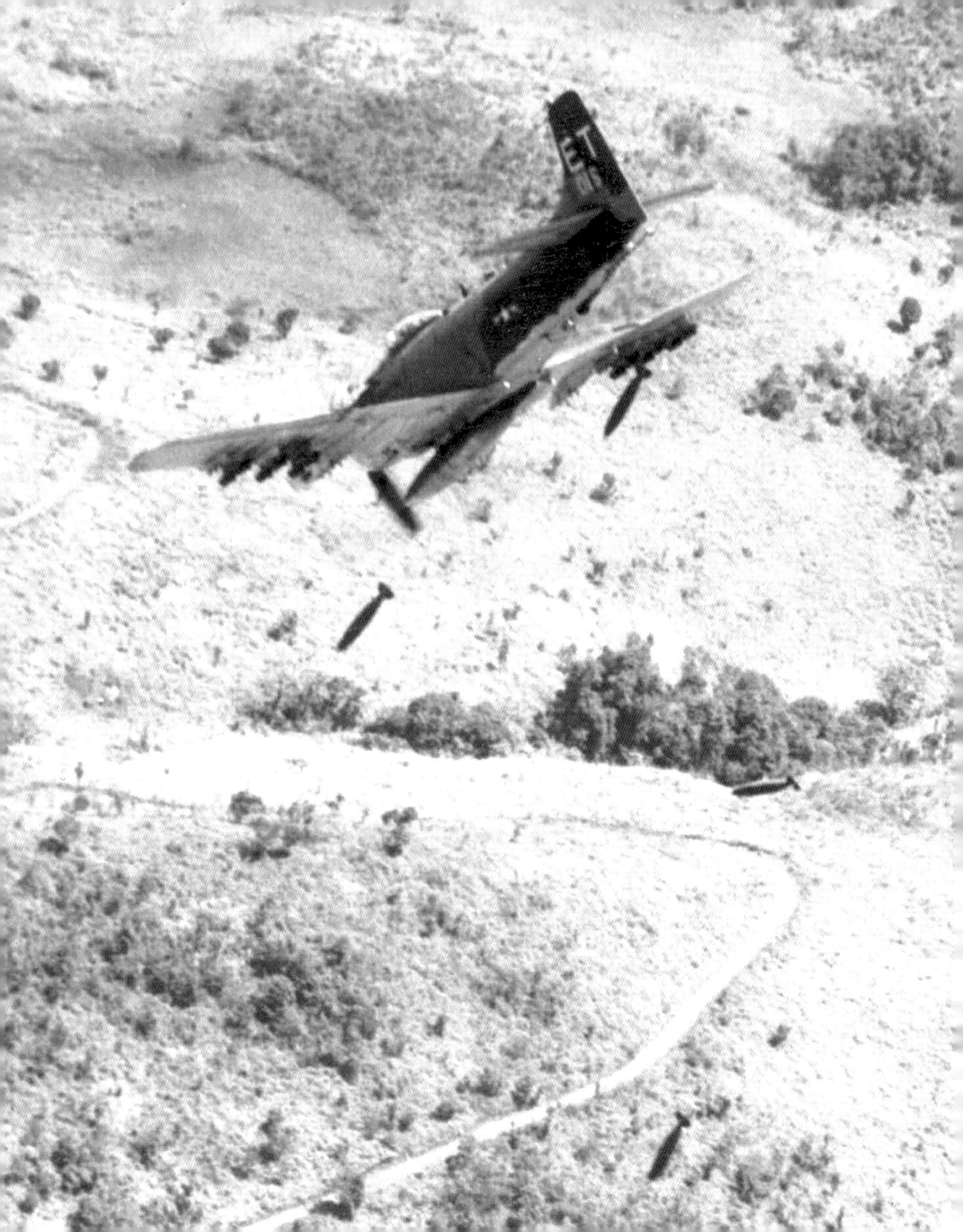

Series Glossary of Key Terms

ARVN Army of the Republic of Vietnam.

Boat People A term given to refugees fleeing Vietnam following the Communist takeover.

Body Count The number of enemy soldiers killed in an engagement.

Charlie, Charles or **Mr Charlie** Slang for the Viet Cong.

Chopper Helicopter.

Containment U.S. government policy to prevent the spread of Communism.

Demilitarized Zone (DMZ) The line that divided North Vietnam and South Vietnam, located at the 17th parallell.

Domino Theory A chain of events describing a situation when one country falls to Communism, others will follow.

DRV Acronym for Democratic Republic of Vietnam.

Friendly Fire An accidental attack on one's own military forces.

Gulf of Tonkin Incident Two attacks by North Vietnam against U.S. destroyers *USS Maddox* and *USS Turner Joy*.

Ho Chi Minh Trail Supply paths used by Communist forces to supply troops fighting in the South.

Irregulars Armed individuals or groups not members of regular armed forces.

Napalm A defoliant chemical dispersed by bombs or flamethrowers, used to destroy foliage in order to expose enemy troops.

Post-traumatic Stress Disorder A psychological disorder caused by experiencing trauma. Symptoms include flashbacks, nightmares, lack of sleep, and other psychological problems.

POW Acronym for prisoner of war.

MIA Acronym for missing in action.

Tet Offensive A large scale attack on South Vietnam by North Vietnam's army and the Viet Cong.

Tonkin Northern section of Vietnam.

Tunnel Rats Soldiers who explored the network of tunnels constructed by the Viet Cong.

Viet Cong Communist guerrilla forces in South Vietnam.

Viet Minh League for the Independence of Vietnam established by Ho Chi Minh.

Vietnamization The process of withdrawing U.S. troops from Vietnam and turning over combat to the South Vietnamese.

Further Reading and Internet Resources

WEBSITES

http://spartacus-educational.com/VietnamWar.htm

http://www.history.com/topics/vietnam-war

https://www.britannica.com/event/Vietnam-War

http://www.historynet.com/vietnam-war

BOOKS

Hourly History. *Vietnam War: A History From Beginning to End,* Hourly History Ltd., 2016. Kindle edition 2016.

Mark Atwood Lawrence. *The Vietnam War: A Concise International History.* Oxford University Press, 2010

Stuart Murray. *DK Eyewitness Books: Vietnam War.* DK Publishing Inc., 2005.

If you enjoyed this book take a look at Mason Crest's other war series:

The Civil War, World War II, Major U.S. Historical Wars.

OVERLEAF
Ho Chi Minh Mausoleum, Hanoi, Vietnam.

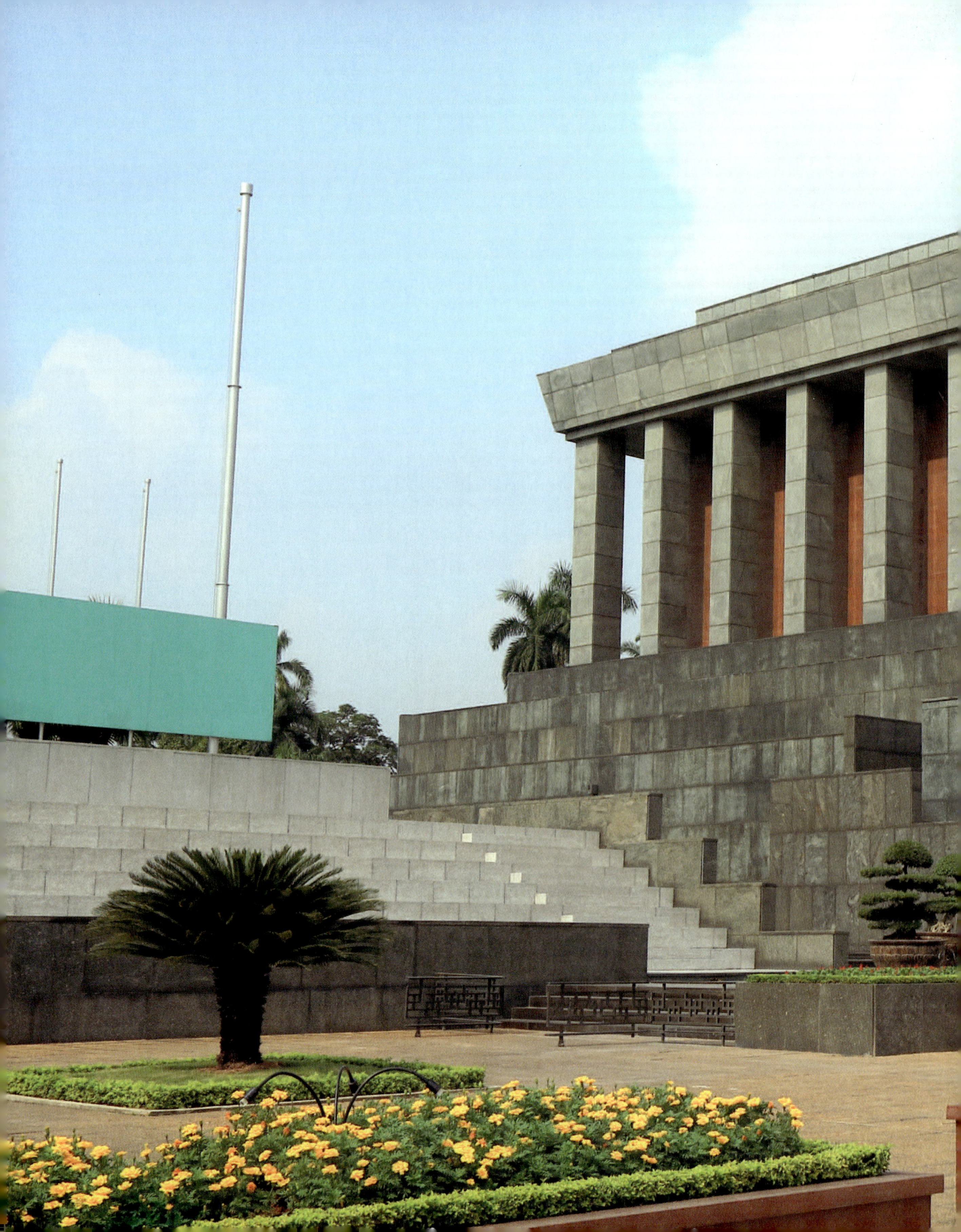

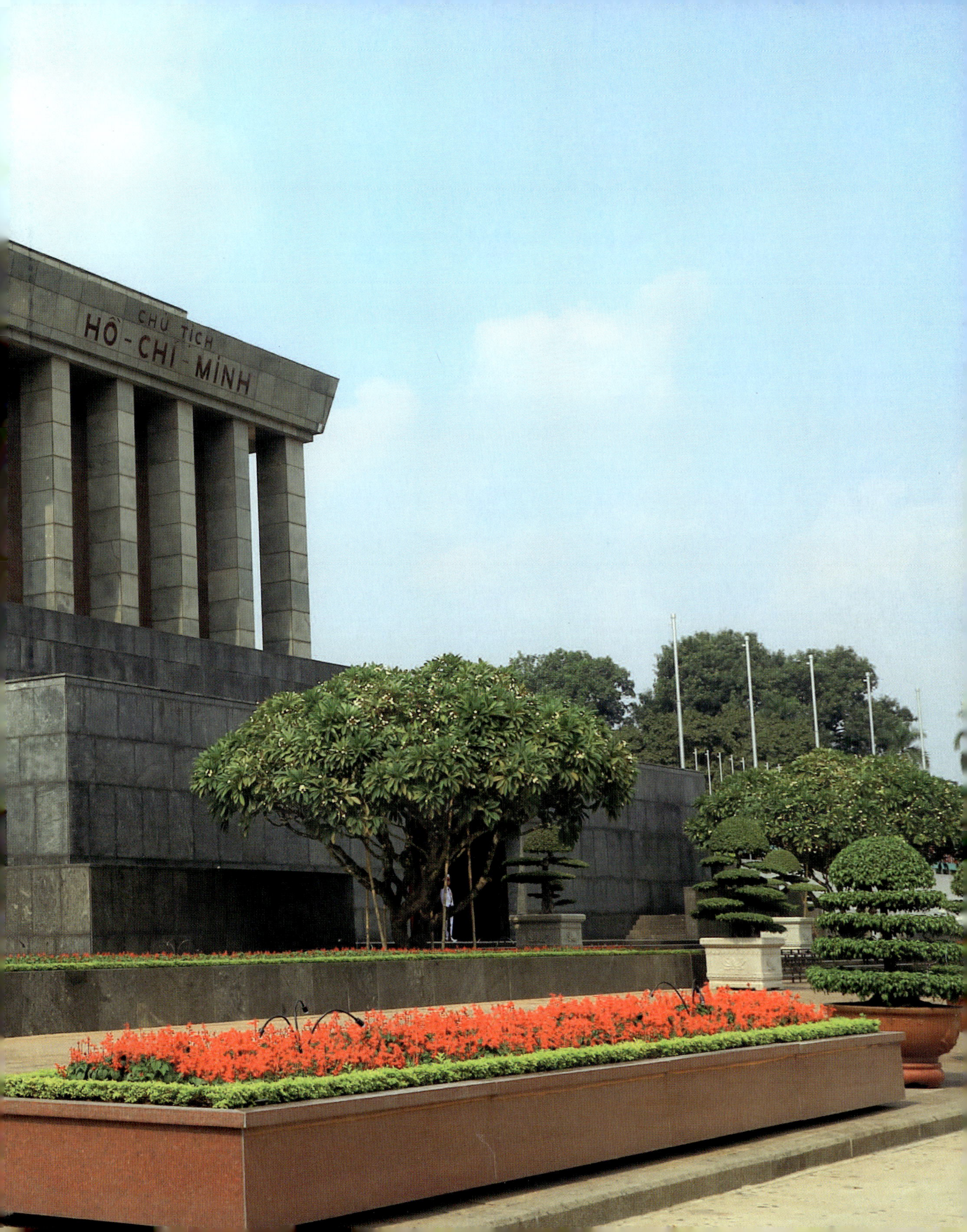
CHỦ TỊCH
HỒ - CHÍ - MINH

Index

Page numbers in ***bold italics*** refer to photographs and their captions or to videos.

A
A-1 Skyraider, *32*, 57, *70–71*
A-1E Skyraider, *38*, 67
A-1J Skyraider, *70–71*
Abrahams, Creighton W., 45
air-mobile operations, 49–50, 51–52, 60
amphibious, definition of, 34
An, General, 65
An Cuong, 37
An Khe Army Airfield, 38–39, *64–65*
An Thuong, 35
Anderson, Dennis K., *24*
Ann-Margret, *45*
Army Aviation School, 41
Australian involvement, 19, 22, *23*, 49
aviation development, 41–42, 44

B
B-52 Stratofortress, 22, 24, 64, 65
Bass, Charles, 66
Bell company, 42
Bien Hoa airfield, 26, *49*
Bong Son district, *32*
booby traps, *17*, *53*
Brown, T. W., 52, 59, 61–62, 65

C
C-130 Hercules, *13*, *66*
Cam Canh Bay, *54*
Cambodia, 69
Camp Hoang Hoa Tham, *60*

casualties, 22, 49, 51, 64–65, 67, 69
CH-47 Chinook, *28–29*, 44
CH-47A Chinook, *31*
CH-53 Sea Stallion, *8–9*
Chen Hoi, 45
Chu Lai, 34–35
Chu Nuy Man, 50, 52, 54
Chu Pong mountains, 51, 52, 54, 64, 65
Cold War, 41
command structure, 19–20
Communist, definition of, 12
counterinsurgency combat operations, 23
Crandall, Bruce P., *56–57*

D
Da Nang Airbase, 12–14, *46–47*, *66*
defoliation missions, *36–37*
Diduryk, Myron, 68
DMZ (demilitarized zone)
    definition of, 12
    strategy and, 30
doctrine, definition of, 34
Dong Nai river, 49
Drang Valley, *56–57*
Duc My Ranger Training Center, *58*

E
enclave strategy, 17, 23

F
Faulks, Billy H., *37*
Forrest, George, 68
Fort Benning, 41, 44, 49
Fort Campbell, *44–45*
Fort Rucker, 41–42
free-fire zones, 33

G
Gaffee, Archie L., *48–49*
Gavin, James M., 41

H
H-21 Shawnee, 47–48
H-34 helicopter, *26–27*
Hall, Lindy R., *16–17*
HAWK surface-to-air missiles, 13
Hester, Curtis E., *37*
Hill 950, *4–5*
HMAS *Hobart*, 19, *19*
HMAS *Perth*, 19, *23*
Ho Chi Minh Mausoleum, *73–75*
Ho Chi Minh Trail
    challenges caused by, 30–31
    description of, 52
    in Laos, 17
    photograph of, *40–41*, *52*
Honest John rockets, 44
Hope, Bob, *45*
Howze Board, 44, 45
Hutton, Carl I., 41

I
Ia Drang, 39, 50, 51–69, *56*
insurgency
    change from, 16
    definition of, 12
international force, deployment of, 16–17
Iron Triangle, *14–15*
Iwo Jima, 38

J
Johnson, Lyndon B.
    counterinsurgency combat operations and, 23–24

deployment authorization from, 14
McNamara and, *35*
proposals presented to, 17
troop increase and, 27
Westmoreland and, 24–25

K
Karsh, Frederick J., 14
Kennedy, John F., *35*
Kinnard, H. W. O., 50
Korean War, 39, 41

L
L-19 Bird Dog, 41
Landing Zone 5, *31*
Laos, 16–17, 69
Lodge, Henry Cabot, 26–27
LZ Albany, 65, 66–69
LZ Columbus, 65, 68
LZ Crooks, 69
LZ Mary, 51
LZ Victor, 59, 62
LZ X-Ray, 52–54, *56*, 62, 65, 68, 69

M
M42A1 Duster, *38–39*
M48 tank, *25*
Marm, Walter J., 56–57, 58–59, 61
McDade, Robert, 65, 66–67, 68
McElroy, Lt. Commander, *4–5*
McNamara, Robert Strange, 17, 26–27, *35*, 42, 44
Military Assistance Command Vietnam (MACV), 12, 20
Moore, H. G., 52–54, 56, 57–58, 59–62, 64–65

More Flags policy, 19

N
Nam Yen Dan Hill 30, 37–38
napalm, *64*
New Zealand, 19, 49
NFL bunker complex, *14*
Ngo Dinh Diem, 22
Nguyen Cao Ky, 24
Nguyen Chanh Thi, 34
Nguyen Quany Canh, *58*
Nguyen Van Thieu, 24
Norodom Sihanouk, Prince, 69
North American F-100D-20-NA Super Sabre, *64*

O
OH-6 helicopters, 51, 52–53
Operation Cedar Falls, *14–15*
Operation Cook, *24*
Operation Eagle Flight, *62*
Operation Prairie III, *16–17*
Operation Rolling Thunder, 12–13, 17, 19
Operation Sea Dragon, *19*
Operation Starlite, 34–35, 37–38
Operation White Wing, *32*

P
Patrol Air Cushion Vehicle (PACV), *38–39*
Payne, D. P., 65–66
Pham Xuan Triem, *58*
Philippines, 19
Platoon Reaction Course, *58–59*
Plei Me, 38–39, 50, 52, 54, 65
Pleiku, 12, 38

Q
Quang Ngai province, *24*
Quat, 24
Qui Nhon, 12

R
Rescorla, Rick, 68
Rich, Charles, 45, 50
Rogers Board, 42
Rumpa, Raymond, *2*, *4*
Rung Sat Special Zone, *18–19*

S
Saigon, *41*, 48
Savage, Sergeant, 60, 61, 62
Scott, James, 66
search-and-destroy missions, 26, 31, *32*, *50–51*
Sharp, Ulysses S. Grant, 14, 20, 22
Slovak, Donald J., 65
Smith, Samuel W., *58*
Smith, Willie C., *12–13*
South Korea, 19
South Vietnamese
  command structure and, 19–20
  corps tactical zones and, 22
  corruption and, 45, 47
  strategy and, 27–28, 30
  Westmoreland and, 24–25
Spain, 19
Sugdinis, Joel, 65
surveillance, definition of, 34

T
T-28, *13*
Taiwan, 19
Tan Son Nhut Airbase, *64*

Index

Tau Nguyen campaign, 50
Taylor, Maxwell, 14, 17, 47
Thailand, 19
Thanh Dien Forest, *14–15*
Thompson, Bill T., *58*
Throckmorton, John, 13
Tolson, John J., 41, 49
Tran Van Vinh, *60*
Tully, Buse, 68
Tully, R. B., 62, 64, 65
Tum Piang Ville, *26*
tunnel complexes, *14–15*

U
UH-1 Iroquois ("Huey"), 42, 44–45
UH-1D helicopter, *36–37*
UH-1D Huey, *42–43*, *56*
USS *Cabildo*, 35
USS *Galveston*, 35
USS *Guadalupe*, *19*
USS *New Jersey*, *45*
USS *Vernon County*, 35, *35*

V
Vam Lang, *54–55*
Van Tuong, 37
Vanderpool, Jay D., 41–42
Viet Cong
 Operation Starlite and, 34–35, 37–38
 prisoners from, *13*, *14–15*, *24*, *34–35*, *62*, *68*
 recruitment and, 23
 in rural areas, 45, 47
 suspects from, *20–21*, *30–31*, *62–63*
Vietnamese Army Jump School, *60*

W
Walt, Lewis William, 34, *35*
Western Highlands Field Front, 50
Westmoreland, William C.
 Brown and, 65
 Central Highlands deployment and, 16, 17
 command structure and, 19–20, 22
 counterinsurgency combat operations and, 23–24
 Da Nang Airbase and, 13–14
 fact-finding mission and, 26–27
 Ho Chi Minh Trail and, 30–31
 An Khe and, 39
 Laos and, 69
 photograph of, *14–15*, *54–55*
 on South Vietnam, 12, 14–15
 strategy and, 16–17, 24–25, 27–28, 30
 Tau Nguyen campaign and, 50
Wheeler, Earle G., 17
Widdifield, Russell R., *3–4*
Williamson, Ellis W., 48–49

Z
Zone D, 26, *50–51*, 53

RIGHT: Members of Troop B, 1st Squadron, 9th Cavalry, 1st Cavalry Division (Airmobile) await orders while a man ahead is clearing and checking the area before the troops enter it. July 1967.

The U.S. Ground War in Vietnam 1965 – 1973

PHOTOGRAPHIC ACKNOWLEDGEMENTS

All images in this book are supplied by Cody Images and are in the public domain.

The content of this book was first published as *VIETNAM WAR*.

ABOUT THE AUTHOR
Christopher Chant

Christopher Chant is a successful writer on aviation and modern military matters, and has a substantial number of authoritative titles to his credit. He was born in Cheshire, England in December 1945, and spent his childhood in East Africa, where his father was an officer in the Colonial Service. He returned to the UK for his education at the King's School, Canterbury (1959–64) and at Oriel College, Oxford (1964–68). Aviation in particular and military matters in general have long been a passion, and after taking his degree he moved to London as an assistant editor on the Purnell partworks, *History of the Second World War* (1968–69) and *History of the First World War* (1969–72). On completion of the latter he moved to Orbis Publishing as editor of the partwork, *World War II* (1972–74), on completion of which he decided to become a freelance writer and editor.

Living first in London, then in Lincolnshire after his marriage in 1978, and currently in Sutherland, at the north-western tip of Scotland, he has also contributed as editor and writer to the partworks, *The Illustrated Encyclopedia of Aircraft*, *War Machine*, *Warplane*, *Take-Off*, *World Aircraft Information Files* and *World Weapons*, and to the magazine *World Air Power Journal*. In more recent years he was also involved in the creation of a five-disk CR-ROM series, covering the majority of the world's military aircraft from World War I to the present, and also in the writing of scripts for a number of video cassette and TV programs, latterly for Continuo Creative.

As sole author, Chris has more than 90 books to his credit, many of them produced in multiple editions and co-editions, including more than 50 on aviation subjects. As co-author he has contributed to 15 books, ten of which are also connected with aviation. He has written the historical narrative and technical database for a five-disk *History of Warplanes* CD-ROM series, and has been responsible for numerous video cassette programs on military and aviation matters, writing scripts for several TV programmes and an A–Z 'All the World's Aircraft' section in Aerospace/Bright Star *World Aircraft Information Files* partwork. He has been contributing editor to a number of books on naval, military and aviation subjects as well as to numerous partworks concerned with military history and technology. He has also produced several continuity card sets on aircraft for publishers such as Agostini, Del Prado, Eaglemoss, Edito-Service and Osprey.